C000165502

Praise for

LARGE AND
IN CHARGE
NO MORE

"Mike Milano's book on vulnerability is a must add to all leaders' professional libraries. In his book Mike talks, with great detail and poignant stories, on how to be a more effective leader by practicing, at the appropriate time, vulnerability. Reading this book, and putting into practice his thoughts and ideas, have made me a better leader. It will for you as well."

—RICK LYNCH
   Lieutenant General, US Army (Retired)
   President/CEO, R Lynch Enterprises, LLC

"Leaders who exhibit strength alone can evoke confidence in their followers. But leaders who exhibit both strength and vulnerability can evoke much more. This powerful combination can elicit not only confidence but imitation, affection, adulation, and even love in others. General Mike Milano makes a very persuasive case that leaders hoping to expand a greater human connection with their followers can do so by putting their innate vulnerability on display along with their strength."

—PATRICK C. FRIMAN, PH.D., ABPP
   Vice President of Behavioral Health, Boys Town

"This book is a real-life roadmap for how to lead with vulnerability, course correct when necessary, see the potential in everyone, and get back up when things don't go as planned."

—LEAH M. BROWN
   Executive Leadership Coach,
   Certified Daring to Lead™ Facilitator

LARGE AND IN CHARGE NO MORE

LARGE AND IN CHARGE NO MORE

A Journey to Vulnerable Leadership

MIKE MILANO

Major General US Army (Ret.)

with HOLLY RICHMOND

For information about this title or to order other books
and/or electronic media, contact the publisher:

MG (R) Mike Milano
www.milanoleadershipservices.com
james.m.milano@gmail.com

ISBNs:
979-8-9875143-2-0 (hardcover)
979-8-9875143-0-6 (softcover)
979-8-9875143-1-3 (eBook)

Printed in the United States of America

Cover and interior design by 1106 Design

Dedicated to all those who serve.

ACKNOWLEDGMENTS

There are many people to whom I owe an enormous debt of gratitude for their contributions, efforts, encouragement, and guidance in this endeavor. Without my co-author Holly Richmond's insights, diligence, patience, and expertise, this project might not have happened. Thanks for your willingness to work with me—I know it wasn't always easy. You've been a real pro, and I realize you've put off your own writing projects to do this with me.

To my friend and mentor, Lieutenant General (Retired) Rick Lynch, thank you for the idea to write this book, for your persistent nudging to get it done, your guidance, your promotion, your helpful feedback, and, of course, your endorsement of my work. You've been a source of inspiration and emulation to me for the 35 years I've known you.

Several other accomplished professionals took time out of their busy schedules to read the manuscript and provide invaluable feedback as well as their endorsement—special thanks to Vince DePalma, Dr. Pat Friman, Gen (Retired) Stan McChrystal, Major General (Retired) Will Grimsley, and Leah Brown.

Special thanks to Marie Hansen, Rita Paskowitz, and Heidi Sell, three extraordinary writers who provided insightful feedback chapter by chapter. Your help was of enormous value.

To my wife, Kim, what can I say? You continue to be my guiding light, my steadying hand, my role model, my biggest supporter, and my most trusted critic. Thanks for your support and encouragement all along the way.

Finally, to all the people I served with during my Army career and in my time with Target, people who made an impact on my life based on your leadership influence, your guidance and direction, your friendship, your feedback, and most importantly, your vulnerability. I am deeply indebted to you all and am forever grateful.

CONTENTS

INTRODUCTION

Humidity hung in the air thick as a rug. Still mid-morning on an ordinary July day in 1995, the sun beat down on Fort Stewart, Georgia. I was a lieutenant colonel in the United States Army, commanding a tank battalion. We stood on the parade field dressed in our camouflage Battle Dress Uniforms, or BDUs, under a cloudless sky with only an occasional sigh of wind, not enough to ripple the array of unit colors—or flags—which hung limply from their staffs. Behind me, standing at attention, were my four primary staff officers, and behind them about 180 of the roughly 500 men in my battalion. In front of us, spectators in the bleachers fanned programs in front of their faces as the change-of-command ceremony proceeded for my direct superiors, the incoming and outgoing brigade commanders. Only a month before, I had assumed command of the tank battalion I was leading that day.

Ceremonies have been part of military culture for thousands of years. These traditions are conducted for all sorts of reasons—to honor fallen comrades, to celebrate national holidays or other commemorations, and to mark the change of command from one leader to another. The purpose of a change-of-command ceremony is to thank a unit's outgoing commander and his spouse for their leadership and contributions and to welcome the new commanding couple. During the ceremony, the unit is showcased one last time for the outgoing commander and for the first time for the incoming one.

Like many of these ceremonies, the pageantry is thrilling. The national anthem is played by a marching band, as the unit colors and flags are brought forward in front of the bleachers. Troops are inspected, snapping to attention as the reviewing party—the two commanders and their superior—march past. Soldiers execute a series of precise movements in response to specific commands issued by their leaders. Seeing hundreds and sometimes thousands of soldiers, colors flying, move in sync with perfect choreography can be quite moving. As they march in formation past the reviewing stand at the end of the ceremony, they are a source of great pride for both incoming and outgoing commanders and the assembled gathering of attendees.

The sequence of a change-of-command ceremony includes assembling the troops and then an invocation or benediction. Spouses are recognized and given flowers, and after the command has been transferred to the new commander, speeches are given focusing on the accomplishments of the outgoing commander. Finally, brief comments are made by the incoming commander, who typically talks about how proud he is to lead America's finest. Many times, these speeches are inspiring because they highlight the work of the entire command and praise the hard work done by those in silent formation on the field.

Standing in front of my battalion, listening to the remarks being made by my leaders that day, I began to sweat profusely, more than typical for the normally muggy weather. My head suddenly felt as light as a balloon. I started shaking. I couldn't maintain my stance and staggered a bit. One of my staff officers behind me asked, in a bare whisper, "Are you all right, sir?"

I began to panic. I felt the eyes of everyone zeroing in on me—the spectators in the stands, the troops behind me, the outgoing and incoming commander and their boss, and the presiding officer for the ceremony. I realized there was no possibility that my actions would go unnoticed. I felt my knees begin to buckle and knew I wouldn't be able to remain standing. I stumbled to the back of the formation, and my executive officer, or second-in-command, stepped into my position. I bent over, flexed my knees, and took deep breaths—everything I could to get myself back to normal.

Change-of-command ceremonies usually last about an hour, and it's not unusual for a soldier every now and then to "fall out" or break ranks during the course of the event. It happens for any number of reasons. Sometimes, they lock their knees and prevent the flow of blood to their heads, or they might be suffering from dehydration. Or they might fall out for lack of sleep or too much drink the night before. Standing still for an hour takes practice.

However, a commander falling out is never good for any reason.

After a few minutes, I returned to my position in front of the formation. My executive officer gave me a pleading look that said, "Are you sure, sir?" But I insisted, determined to fulfill my role, and made it through the rest of the ceremony without incident.

To say I was embarrassed is an understatement. I was mortified. From the day I entered ROTC in college, and during my subsequent 16 years of leading soldiers, it was drummed into me that a leader in the Army sets an example for his men; he shows no weakness, indecision, or lack of judgment. Clearly, falling out didn't fit that mantra. I searched for a cause. I was in excellent health and in great physical condition, with the exception of genetic high blood pressure, which I believed was under control with medication. I wondered if my episode had had something to do with that. Maybe the dosage wasn't right. Could it have caused me to be hypotensive and lightheaded? Or, could it have been performance anxiety? Maybe, but I'd never experienced anything like it during the countless other ceremonies I'd taken part in.

That evening, we held a social gathering for the unit at a local establishment, as we occasionally did to welcome new arrivals and bid farewell to those leaving the battalion. A subtle sense of unease seemed to permeate the roomful of officers, senior noncommissioned officers, and their spouses. I couldn't help feeling my falling out was the 800-pound gorilla in the room.

I had to get up and kick off the evening's events. Usually, I have no problem poking fun at myself or enjoying a laugh at my expense, but that evening, I stood and addressed what had taken place head-on. I didn't pretend it hadn't happened or make light of falling out. I apologized, vowed it wouldn't happen again, and said I'd work to fix any damage I might have caused to the reputation of the battalion. To my surprise, my openness, my taking responsibility, lightened the atmosphere. Afterward, some people told me they were impressed at how honest I'd been.

Although my superiors seemed satisfied with my response, in my mind, I was still obsessed about it. I thought I had damaged my career and my credibility as a leader.

That turned out not to be the case.

Immediately after relinquishing my two-year battalion command, the conventional duration of a command tour, I was selected to attend the prestigious Army War College in Carlisle,

Pennsylvania. That year at Carlisle was followed by a plum job as a division G3, the most difficult of all staff-officer positions. I was given the responsibility for all operations, plans, and training for a 25,000-soldier division deploying to Bosnia-Herzegovina. It appeared my faux pas on the marching field hadn't hurt me after all. Subconsciously, I breathed a sigh of relief and tried to put the incident behind me.

Five years later, in the summer of 2000, shortly after taking command of a brigade combat team as a full colonel, it happened again—even more dramatically. On another warm July morning, this time at Fort Riley, in eastern Kansas, I stood in front of about 200 of my approximately 5,000 troops. Beside me stood a soldier with my brigade's colors, campaign streamers resplendently representing all the combat action it had been part of in its impressive history. We were the 1st Brigade, 1st Infantry Division—the storied Big Red One—one of the most legendary and highly decorated divisions in the Army. Created in 1917 as the first division formed to fight in World War I, it has always been highly respected. Commanding its 1st Brigade was a dream come true for me, a truly prestigious command.

The change of command that day was for a two-star general who was handing command of our division over to another two-star general, as well as the entire Fort Riley installation— one of the Army's crown jewels. Presiding over the events was a three-star general. A few hundred people filled the stands—the installation's leadership, their spouses, local dignitaries, guests of the two-star generals, and fellow commanders. This was the place to be at Fort Riley that July morning.

The ceremony began. The order "Center, March" was given to the formation of officers and their associated colors on the field. We executed sharp facing movements and marched crisply forward to a position immediately in front of the reviewing stand, where both two-star generals and the presiding three-star waited. Once we were in place, the band played a rousing national anthem. The generals came forward and carried out the ritual exchanging of the division's colors, passing them from one to the other to signify that leadership had, in fact, been transferred, and that we now had a new leader on board. With a quick about-face, the generals returned to the reviewing platform.

During the following speeches, we remained at attention in front of the stand, while the rest of the troops on the field were ordered to stand at parade rest. Soldiers standing at parade rest are told to make imperceptible micro-movements with their bodies, especially their legs, to keep the blood flowing and ensure they don't lock up. Although this can be done when at attention (a much more rigid stance), it is more of an art, especially when standing so close to so many eyes. I clearly had not mastered this technique.

Shortly after the speeches began, I fell over like a sack of gravel being tossed off the back of a pickup truck. The last words I heard were, "So great to be here at Fort Riley, accompanied by this beautiful azure sky . . ."

When I hit the ground, my helmet nearly fell off my head, despite my chin strap. I was briefly out cold. I lay in a crumpled heap, and two medics who had been in the vicinity of the reviewing stand ran onto the field. They loosened my clothing, checked my pulse, and talked to me calmly in low, steady voices when I came to. They helped me up with the intention of walking me off the field. But again, I refused.

I shook my head to clear it, awkwardly reset my helmet on top of my head, and straightened my uniform. I stepped back into position. All the while, the speeches continued as if nothing out of the ordinary was occurring in front of the reviewing stand. When I looked forward, though, I could see hundreds of eyes on me. No one had missed the incident—I was front and center along with the other leaders. I could almost hear them thinking, "What the hell? Brigade commanders don't do that. Is he even fit to lead a brigade? How long before he goes over again?" I took a quick glance at my wife, Kim, and until this day, I can still see the empathetic anguish on her face.

I managed to complete the rest of the ceremony. I marched with authority as I led my assembled soldiers past the reviewing stand for the portion of the ceremony called the "Pass in Review." All the while my mind raced, thinking every eye was following me, waiting for me to trip up again and sprawl indecorously on the neatly clipped parade field.

Later that afternoon, when I met with my staff and subordinate commanders, I felt less than capable of being the leader they expected. For the second time in five years, I was completely mortified and thought my career, if not over, had been damaged in some way. Once again, I addressed the issue head-on, acknowledged my misstep, and told my subordinates I would do everything in my power not to let them down again. I told them I was sorry I had embarrassed them and had tarnished the reputation of the great brigade with which I'd been entrusted.

I analyzed what might have caused the episode. I looked again at adjusting my blood-pressure medication—I hadn't had to do so five years earlier, but perhaps something had changed. I suspected that, anxious about the previous incident at Fort Stewart, I might have been overthinking what my body would do standing at attention for an extended period of time. Perhaps a bout of performance anxiety? I worked with my brother-in-law, Dr. Pat Friman, a behavioral psychologist, who coached me on mental techniques I could employ to calm my mind. He showed me how to teach myself to accept what was happening in my body rather than fight it. I believe these things worked. I never had to adjust my medication, and I never fell out again through the innumerable ceremonies I participated in or led during the rest of my career.

However, everything this second time had been doubled—the ceremony more prestigious, my falling out more glaring, my embarrassment more scorching, my determination to prevent another occurrence more urgent, and my worry about my career more gnawing. But despite these fears, my career was not impacted. My next assignment was an excellent job in the Pentagon, one that was essential to be considered for promotion to brigadier general. In fact, I was selected for promotion less than two years later during my stint at the Pentagon, at a relatively young age, compared to the rest of my newly promoted cohort.

Throughout the rest of my career, however, I carried around a nugget of shame. In my mind, these incidents were black marks on my record of leadership. I buried them deep, as we all do with shameful things we'd rather not think about. But subconsciously, there was always a niggling thought that maybe I wasn't leadership material. Why hadn't I been able to physically—or maybe psychologically—stand at attention like the other officers and the color guards on the field? Did it say something about my character? I suspect I made more of these incidents than was warranted, but still, I couldn't shake this doubt.

Years later, after retiring from the Army and spending some time as a corporate leader, I pondered the elusive question of what makes someone an effective leader. I dredged up these episodes in my Army career and looked at them in a different light.

On those parade fields on those two infamous, inglorious days, I had exhibited behavior that was the opposite of what I had been taught a strong leader should show. Yes, they were just ceremonies, and no soldiers under my responsibility were injured or lost their lives. But in my mind, I had been weak and vulnerable in the worst kind of way at the wrong time. And yet, contrary to what I believed, the news of my two incidents was not widespread. I had suffered no detrimental effects, except for some good-natured ribbing—and perhaps silent gloating—from other officers competing with me for promotion. My career had bloomed, not withered.

If showing weakness was a sign of a poor leader, how was that possible?

It occurred to me that maybe how I'd handled my two moments of extreme vulnerability had something to do with it. I did not let my weakness stop me from getting back in line and completing my role in those ceremonies. I did not pretend the incidents didn't happen. I did not blame them on circumstances. I did not blame them on a misstep or the heat of the day or someone else. While every fiber of my body wanted to make those events go away, I immediately confessed the truth of the matter to my peers and subordinates. I acknowledged my fallibility and my desire to improve. I took responsibility for preventing similar incidents from happening again—I *owned* them.

And, going forward, I felt more compassionate toward my subordinates. If appropriate, in all the ceremonies I conducted later in my career after Fort Riley, I told the commanders and soldiers on the field to take off their helmets, shake their limbs a bit, flex their knees, and then get back into formation to continue the proceedings. This was unconventional, for sure, but I'd seen other leaders do the same, and it felt empathetic and heartfelt to me. In other words, my action after my two moments of painful vulnerability had been to *remain vulnerable*.

This is vulnerability of the best kind.

This realization gave me pause. It made me think that, although we were all programmed in the Army to believe that good leaders are strong, confident, and unerring, maybe the truth lay elsewhere. Maybe the key to good leadership was counterintuitive. Maybe good leadership had nothing to do with the outward toughness and confidence we show the world, but rather had more to do with a way of being that embraces and acknowledges humans as imperfect beings. *And* that leaders, *especially*, need to show this side of themselves to be effective.

Obviously, I didn't understand this at the time. My response to falling-out had been instinctual and could just as easily have gone differently. Which brings me to the reason I am writing this book. It seems to me that it is time to make vulnerability a part of every discussion about leadership. To make vulnerability a well-worn, skillfully wielded tool in every leader's toolbox.

‹ ◂ ◆ ▸ ›

WHAT DOES VULNERABLE LEADERSHIP MEAN?

Vulnerability is the main building block of good leadership

When I retired from the Army in 2012 as one of roughly 300 general officers on active duty, I considered my 33-year military career a highly successful one by any measure. I thought I had the "leadership thing" sorted out. However, shortly after retiring, I took a position with Target Corporation as a Senior Director, Distribution. I'd been brought in to run a large regional distribution center in DeKalb, Illinois. Initially, our 500 team members were responsible for supporting about 70 stores in 5 Midwestern states, but over time, we transformed our supply chain role and grew to support about 700 stores in 19 states.

From the start, it became clear that the expectations for leaders at Target were different from those in the Army. Target desired leaders who participated, encouraged input from different sources, partnered with others, and created a collaborative atmosphere. Most important, Target leaders were expected to understand and operate effectively within its culture, one that emphasized engagement, collaboration, and inclusion. They encouraged leaders to admit they didn't have all the answers, that there was room for improvement and growth—and space to be vulnerable.

This was different from my experience as a leader in the Army. From the lowest tactical echelon to the largest military formations, it was inculcated—a cultural norm—that leaders were individuals who were "large and in charge," especially in the combat-arms branches. Leaders were decisive, confident, competent, courageous, and out front leading the way. The Infantry motto *is* "Follow Me!" after all. Army leaders were expected to inspire their troops to accomplish any and all missions by setting an example for their troops to follow, sometimes at the risk of life and limb. With this strong, unerring, bold kind of leader, it was assumed that others would naturally follow and that the whole outfit would be successful. In this leadership dynamic, there was little room for vulnerability—and understandably so. Combat situations typically don't afford a leader the luxury of being vulnerable; lives are often at stake, and mission accomplishment hinges on split-second decision-making and decisiveness.

Still, this culture meant that, even in peacetime, leaders weren't encouraged to admit they didn't have all the answers, that they might be fearful and uncertain about the way ahead, or that they needed input from subordinates. In the everyday operations of the Army, from meetings to briefings to some of the more mundane tasks that make up any organization, this rugged leadership model stubbornly clung. Rank certainly had a lot to do with it. Rank and hierarchy permeate all military interactions. Unless an order or directive from a superior is illegal, immoral, or unethical, recipients are duty-bound to do their best to execute that order, whether or not they agree with it.

This is not to say that disagreement was rare or that moral courage was lacking. On the contrary, good leaders often sought input from advisors and subject-matter experts. But ultimately, the decisions of those in charge carried the day, and compliance with those decisions was the cultural expectation. I can recall countless times that suggestions or even disagreements were met with the half-humorous, snarky reply, "I appreciate your interest in national security—now execute what I said to do."

The Army wasn't alone in espousing this approach to leadership. Across all swathes of American culture over the last hundred years, our nation has embraced great leaders who present the image of being unflinching and strong. We've idolized the individual rather than the team. We've rewarded those who take bold positions and stand their ground. One has only to look at our movies, obsession with sports, political representation, and celebrity culture to understand the type of leaders our culture tells us we should admire. It is not surprising that, in all aspects of life for so many years, the idea of leadership looked much like the model I experienced in the Army.

Although a new paradigm of leadership is emerging, it often clashes with these leadership conceptions of the past that were ingrained in most of us since childhood. Our society and our parents modeled this type of behavior for us.

My mother was a stay-at-home Mom. My father, born and raised in Chicago in a modest but comfortable neighborhood, was a businessman in marketing and sales who ended up running his own company. He was the grandson of Italian immigrants who came to America in the late 1800s. His father was an electrician with the local utility, his mother was the office manager for a large real-estate company executive, and my father was the first in his family to go to college under the GI Bill. He took full advantage of that generous governmental program, which enabled hundreds of thousands of veterans to go to college, even though he later vehemently supported the position that everyone else should pull themselves up by their own bootstraps.

His philosophy was to win at all costs, crush every opponent, and secure as much wealth and status as he could. He went where the opportunities and money were, and we moved 10 times before I graduated from high school. I attended six different schools—five during my 6th- through 12th-grade years. My father, not an altogether uncaring man, didn't spend a lot of time considering the impact on his family of these frequent moves. He was the family leader, and he knew best. Making more money and getting promoted justified disrupting our lives, education, friendships, schools, and opportunities to fit into social groups.

He was typical of many head-of-the-family businessmen back then. He was a white, middle-class, heterosexual man who spent most of his time working, touting his achievements, telling others what to do, and dominating social situations, while his wife dutifully handled the domestic environment in a way that caused him the minimum amount of trouble.

My father was probably the least vulnerable person I've ever encountered, although, of course, I loved him and learned a lot from him. Always the loudest person in the room, the life of the party, a true extrovert, a talented salesman, and good-looking, he never seemed satisfied. Something always wasn't quite right. Blessed with a good intellect, ambition, a dedicated wife, and healthy and resilient children, he couldn't seem to appreciate what he had. A nice home? He'd begrudgingly call it okay and then immediately find some fatal flaw that typically generated another move. As a result, we were uprooted when we didn't need to be.

My dad was a classic example of a man desiring to be wealthier than "the Joneses." He needed a new car every year or two, belonged to country clubs, and used status symbols for one-upmanship and as a means to demonstrate his worth.

This was my role model for what a successful business leader looked like. No doubt, my father learned this from his own role models who were, interestingly, blue-collar workers, except for his father-in-law, who was a successful salesman who'd gone to school only through the 8th grade. Perhaps the role model he admired most was his Uncle Jim, who served in the Coast Guard and participated in amphibious activity during World War II, including operating a Landing Ship Tank (LST) at the battle of Iwo Jima.

My father encouraged me never to show weakness, never back down, and never give an inch. When I was young, he often came home after work and talked to my mom over drinks, bragging about how *he'd told so and so to shove it up his ass, that he wasn't taking any shit from anyone.* He even got fired once for telling his boss at the A.C. Nielsen company to go screw himself. I remember that, once, when I was in 7th grade, a kid picked on my younger brother, John, and my father thought I should have done more to come to my brother's aid. He gave me an earful about that and boasted how, as a kid, he'd stuck up for his own younger brother by smashing the other guy in the face. What mattered to my father and many others of their generation was the tough-guy, savvy dealmaker, and wealthy-pillar-of-the-community persona he presented to the world. He saw no hypocrisy in how his day-to-day behavior didn't always match this crafted persona.

When I was in eighth grade, the movie *Patton* came out, about General George S. Patton, a brilliant Army strategist and rugged individualist who inspired his troops with his grit, courage, and chutzpah. Not surprisingly, my dad loved it. Here was a protagonist who knew more than his superiors, wasn't afraid to speak his mind, and never backed down. My father's adoration of Patton rubbed off on me and planted in my mind the seed of what an Army officer should be.

When I think back about two other films that were the rage at the time—*Butch Cassidy and the Sundance Kid*, a film about two outlaws who outwit law enforcement, and *Bullitt*, a film about an all-guts police detective in San Francisco who defies politicians to bring down a mob boss—the protagonists are all individualistic tough guys who gain the grudging admiration of others by excelling in wit and courage without showing any weakness. Is it any wonder that a whole generation of young men entered the workforce thinking that a leader should know everything, be one step ahead of everyone else, and be invincible?

Even in sports, where the idea of teamwork is introduced to children, there are mixed messages. As a young kid in California, I participated in the state's well-run youth baseball organization. My Dad was the coach. In contrast to much of the way my father approached life, he turned out to be a great coach. He did his best to instill in me the importance of teamwork. He told me that just because I was the coach's son, I would get no preferential treatment, and he held good to his word. But throughout all levels of sports, there is also encouragement to conform to an underlying *star mentality*—to strive to be the one individual that stands out. Heroes are never just solid team players. They are always the individuals with exceptional talent. My heroes as a kid were all the greats—Sandy Koufax, Bobby Orr, John Havlicek, Walt Frazier, and Carl Yastrzemski. These "heroes" were assumed to be good leaders, even if they weren't, just because they had mastered the game.

It is always hard to alter the ingrained notions society has given us, but the world changes, and to be successful, our ideas have to conform to new ways. That includes notions about leadership. Changes in technology, the workplace, and the global climate mean the skills people bring to work are changing, and leaders must adapt. Today, our workforces are more diverse and skill sets more complicated—no one person understands every aspect of the work. Not everyone works in the same place anymore. Technology has allowed us to communicate in different ways, broaden competition, and demand quicker reaction times.

A search for the kind of skills future leaders will need brings up many articles listing the required traits—qualities such as emotional intelligence, resilience, active agility, adaptability, cultural intelligence, collaboration, cognitive flexibility, vision, courage, and authenticity. Not many of these articles discuss how leaders who have been raised with ingrained outdated conceptions of leadership can develop these new qualities. They simply say they are needed and why. Sure, there is always a whole range of leadership-training programs available. Consultants are ready and available to help corporations adapt to new policies and institute cultural changes. But in my mind, the one essential ingredient that is missing in a lot of discussions about transforming the old leadership paradigm into the new is the need for vulnerability.

Leaders cannot change if they are not willing to be vulnerable.

Perhaps the reticence to use the word "vulnerability" in conjunction with leadership comes from the way our society has viewed that word. *The Merriam-Webster Dictionary* defines "vulnerable" as:

1. capable of being physically or emotionally wounded

2. open to attack or damage: assailable, vulnerable to criticism

A third definition is listed about a position in the game of bridge.

Nowhere does the dictionary define "vulnerability" more positively as a state of openness. This omission reflects the negative connotation "being vulnerable" has in our society. Vulnerability is defined as something *done to* a person, not a state a person can willingly *put themselves into*. People are defined as vulnerable almost exclusively when they are hurt, wounded, damaged, or defenseless—when they are a victim.

In recent years, the idea of vulnerability as a positive state has begun to gain traction. An expert on the subject of vulnerability, Brené Brown, author of *Daring Greatly*, provides this take: "The definition of vulnerability is uncertainty, risk, and emotional exposure. But vulnerability is not weakness; it's our most accurate measure of courage. When the barrier is our belief about vulnerability, the question becomes: 'Are we willing to show up and be seen when we can't control the outcome?' When the barrier to vulnerability is about safety, the question becomes: 'Are we willing to create courageous spaces so we can be fully seen?'" By using the words "are we willing," Brown puts choice in our hands. Vulnerability no longer belongs only to the victim.

Reframing vulnerability this way makes it almost a prerequisite to becoming a good leader. Being responsible for employees, troops, teams, and followers means leaders are also accountable for the work environment, the activities at the workplace, and safety. The article "Today's Leaders Need Vulnerability, Not Bravado" published October 19, 2020, in the *Harvard Business Review*, by Amy C. Edmonson and Tomas Chamorro-Premuzic, describes a vulnerable leader as, ". . . being aware of one's limitations, possessing the necessary humility to grow their and others' potential, and courageous and curious enough to create sincere and open connections with others. They build inclusive team climates with psychological safety that foster constructive criticism and dissent."

When I joined Target in 2012, it was immediately obvious to me that the corporation had made the commitment to shift to this new paradigm and that it was part of its culture. Maintaining it required, and still does, ongoing and continuous active work. Behavioral change is never easy, and changing a mindset created over centuries doesn't happen overnight.

I could immediately see the benefits. Even after spending 33 years embracing the Army's view of leadership and strength, I sensed the power of vulnerability. In fact, I wondered how much more effective the Army could be if it advocated for this trait in its leaders. Could even an organization like the Army enhance its effectiveness if it conducted leader-development programs that dispelled misconceptions of vulnerability, encouraged leaders to be vulnerable, and showed the positive impact of it on those being led?

My father would probably say Patton is rolling over in his grave at even the thought. That the last thing the defenders of our country need to be is a bunch of whiny soldiers, running around with their hearts on their sleeves. But that is not what I mean. I am sure that Patton, at certain points in his career, showed vulnerability—just as I did on those ceremonial parade fields. In looking back over my years in the military, I know I did. But it was unconscious. Perhaps I even regretted it. What I'm advocating here is for leaders to develop a *practice of being vulnerable*—to be *intentional* about it—and to clearly understand when it's appropriate and when it's not.

Like all practices, it requires work and diligence to master the skill. So, let's take a look at ways leaders can intentionally use vulnerability to become better leaders.

‹ ‹ ◆ › ›

-2-

KNOWING YOUR LIMITATIONS

A vulnerable leader doesn't have to know everything

Many inspirational posters tout the importance of people not giving in to their limitations, with slogans such as Richard Bach's, "Argue for your limitations, and sure enough, they're yours." Often, this is taken to mean that one shouldn't admit to having any limitations at all. The traditional portrait discussed in the previous chapter—of strong, all-knowing invincible leaders—supports this. Leaders shouldn't show weakness or lack of knowledge to their subordinates, bosses, or peers.

With vulnerable leadership, however, freely admitting limitations is crucial. It opens the door for forward movement and improves the likelihood of making good decisions.

Sadly, there are many stories where the inability to admit limitations and lack of knowledge has led to disastrous and dangerous decision-making, especially in times of great change. Knowledge is generally gained through experience, and experience occurs in the past. However, past experience is often not useful when technology, culture, science, social policy, and other aspects of life change and there is no precedent. In these times, leaders need to be open to learning and understanding the new terrain so they can make better decisions based on the new knowledge. To do this, leaders must acknowledge their limits and put themselves in the vulnerable position of asking others for help and input.

History books are full of examples of leaders who stubbornly refused to acknowledge their limitations, and the results turned out to be tragic. A perfect example of this occurred during World War I. Undreamed-of new weapons, based on technological advances created by the Industrial Revolution, were introduced to battle. On the ground, modifications to machine guns, artillery, mortars, and rifles made rapid, accurate, and long-range fire more possible. On the sea, submarines, torpedoes, and seaplanes meant enemy ships could be attacked both from below and overhead. In the air, airplanes and zeppelins were used for the first time to surveil enemy territory and drop bombs. Completely innovative weapons like tanks, flamethrowers, poison gas, and grenades were unleashed and wreaked havoc on unsuspecting cavalry and foot soldiers.

The rules of war had clearly changed.

And yet, the Allied armies' leadership approach did not. Again and again, they made the same poor decisions, based not on their new actuality but on past experience. Those decisions resulted in a tremendous loss of life.

Before the introduction of this new war technology, open warfare was the name of the game—the infantry, in drill formation, would break the enemy line across open ground, and the cavalry (the elite soldiers) would gallop their horses forward and swiftly clean up, riding so quickly that they made difficult targets. In World War I, the columns of soldiers and cavalry became sitting ducks, instantly cut down by rapid-fire machine guns and artillery shells, horses shot from beneath riders. Because of these new and improved weapons, combat changed, and open warfare was replaced by trench warfare. Troops had to dig trenches to protect themselves from artillery and mortars until they could charge forward in scattered formation through barbed-wire stretches of land and engage the enemy in incremental stages. It was not glorious or affirming. Trench warfare was a deadly slog. The need for it, though, became quickly and irrefutably clear during the first months of the war.

Even so, more than a year after the war's start, troops were still being unnecessarily slaughtered. Adam Hochschild, in his book *To End All Wars,* describes what the Germans witnessed in September 1915, more than a year into the war, during the battle of Loos.

"The British, according to a German account, moved forward in ten columns, 'each about a thousand men, all advancing as if carrying out a parade-ground drill . . . Never had machine guns had such straight-forward work to do . . . with barrels becoming hot . . . they traversed to and fro along the enemy's ranks; one machine gun alone fired 12,500 rounds that afternoon. The result was devastating. The enemy could be seen falling literally in hundreds, but they continued to march.' Some British officers were mounted on horseback, and so made even more conspicuous targets."

Over the course of the war, the French and British were forced to adapt to trench warfare—no country's army could survive the rate of casualties seen at Loos and other early battlefields. In addition, the French troops mutinied early in 1917 in protest of the slaughter. Even with all that, a year after the mutiny, when the Americans joined the war, American generals repeated the same mistakes the French and British had made. Certain leaders in all three armies never gave up the conviction that open warfare was the right approach and that trench warfare was an anomaly that would eventually disappear. They never acknowledged the limitations of their past experience. Imagine the difference it might have made had the generals listened to the voices within their own ranks demanding they change their tactics.

When the title of "leader" is pinned on an individual, there is an assumption that knowledge and expertise come with it. This is an impossible expectation in a changing world and an impossible expectation for any leader thrust into an unfamiliar situation. But even today, instead of training new leaders to openly acknowledge their understandable limitations, it is drilled into them to "fake it until they make it."

Upon graduation from college, with an ROTC-based commission as an officer in the United States Army, and before my first operational assignment, I attended the Army's Chemical Officer Basic Course and learned how to be a non-combat-arms officer. I was given the basics on how to be a successful chemical platoon leader and to incorporate nuclear-, biological-, and chemical-defense measures into combat tactics and plans.

At the time, the Army branches were divided into three groups—combat-arms units (infantry, armor, artillery), combat-support units (engineers, air defense, signal, etc.), and combat service-support units (chemical, sustainment, finance, personnel, etc.). With my training, I belonged to the third category. However, the installation I was assigned to also had a requirement that, before non-combat-arms officers joined their basic branch unit, they had to lead in a combat-arms unit for six months. It made sense for officers who would be supporting combat units to understand the complexities, challenges, and demands these units faced. As a result, my first assignment as a brand-new 2nd lieutenant was to the 2nd Armored Division at Fort Hood, Texas, to serve as a tank platoon leader for six months.

Obviously, I knew nothing about tanks—how they were used or how they fit into the bigger picture of companies and battalions. I can still remember the abject trepidation I felt standing in front of a platoon of seasoned combat-arms soldiers for the first time. What did I know, a recent college graduate not even in the same branch, a "support toad," in the parlance of the time? No one had high expectations of me, a temporary officer just filling in, but I still felt like an outlier, someone yet to earn their credibility.

A few weeks after my arrival, I took my platoon—five tanks— out to conduct maneuver training. On a cold and drizzly Texas day in January, I sat in the tight confines of the tank, my first field ride in an armored vehicle. For the weeks leading up to the exercise, I'd worked with my platoon sergeant to put together the training plan and logistics—arranging for food, fuel, ammunition blanks, and pyrotechnic devices fixed to the tank's main gun that simulated actual firing during training exercises. I had done my best to make sure I hadn't overlooked anything.

Part of the plan included linking up with a senior lieutenant, the support platoon leader, a rank above me, who had the important job of supplying the entire battalion with fuel and ammo. When we pulled into the link-up point, he was waiting for us. With a puzzled look on his face, he told me he'd been trying to call me on the radio, but had received no response. At the time, each tank was equipped with a radio about the size of a small suitcase with twelve programmable pushbuttons. It allowed the platoon leader to communicate on two different frequencies—one for company command and one to communicate between the platoon tanks—with a switch to flip from one frequency to the other. I shook my head. I hadn't been able to hear him.

He frowned and asked if he could look at the radio. Within minutes, he diagnosed the problem. The frequencies had to be changed every day and the pushbuttons reprogrammed. I had set the wrong frequencies. He gave me a quick course on how to do it correctly. My ears turned red in embarrassment. In a tank, communication is essential. Without it, you're lost. My first training mission, and I'd botched it up before it started.

I quickly realized no amount of *faking it* would earn anyone's respect. Tanks are formidable weapons and can be extremely dangerous to operate, fire, and maneuver. A lot can go wrong. My ego and idea of myself as a leader had to be balanced against the safety of my men. I knew I had to ask for help. I thanked him and asked if I could use him as a resource. Fortunately, the support platoon leader was a generous man, without judgment. A couple of years older than me, he'd been in the armor branch since graduating from West Point and had gone to Army Ranger school. We became good friends, and he taught me much about how to be a good tank platoon leader, knowledge that would have been hard to learn on my own.

Not only did I need his help, but I also had to trust my platoon sergeant, the senior noncommissioned officer in the platoon and my principal leadership partner, to show me the ropes. This is always a vulnerable proposition—to maintain a leadership position while acknowledging that your subordinate knows more than you do. Often people conflate not knowing something with abdicating authority, but the two are not necessarily connected. As I learned during those six months at Fort Hood, authority can be built without a wealth of technical knowledge.

I solicited my platoon sergeant's thoughts on just about everything. He'd been in the Army for seven or eight years, had achieved the rank of Staff Sergeant, and knew the job inside and out. He spent a lot of his spare time with me. He advised me on all aspects of my job—planning, logistics, soldier preparedness, equipment maintenance, and tactics. He made sure the soldiers were trained and knew their individual jobs. He helped figure out when and where we needed to refuel; he knew what to do when a tank acted up and how best to do field maintenance on them. He also handled all soldier issues. It was the early 1980s, and the Army was experiencing recruiting challenges, so it wasn't unusual for there to be disciplinary problems.

One morning, he greeted me with a salute. "Sir," he said, "after formation this morning, I conducted a room inspection, checking the field uniforms and gear for the upcoming exercise. Once again, Private Smith's room was a disaster. He's missing personal gear. Claims it was stolen when he was out the other night. I personally don't believe that allegation. This isn't the first time we've had problems with him. I've worked with him as best I could without improvement. I propose we recommend Smith for punishment with an Article 15."

Article 15 allows a company commander to impose punishment such as restrictions, docking pay, or demotion for minor violations. My platoon sergeant waited a moment and then added, "This good?"

Without hands-on knowledge about the soldier, I'd have been an idiot to argue with his recommendation. I agreed.

It turned out that, during the Article 15 proceedings, carried out by the company commander in his office, which my platoon sergeant and I attended, Smith admitted to lying about his equipment getting stolen. He'd sold it because he was broke. This escalated the seriousness of his offense and resulted in Smith getting the maximum punishment allowable—two weeks' restriction, forfeiture of a month's pay, and a reduction in rank from private second class to private (he'd been in the Army about ten months). Afterward, Smith continued to have problems with basic discipline and was a substandard soldier, so he was discharged from the Army with a General Discharge (not an Honorable one) about two months later. He just wasn't cut out to be a soldier, and too much leadership time was needed to keep him straight—time we didn't have to spare.

In this way, with each day-to-day decision, my platoon sergeant taught me what I needed to know to be an effective platoon leader. Although there were some embarrassing moments in being so vulnerable—in being a leader who didn't have the necessary fundamental technical knowledge for his job—I learned two important things.

The first is that loyalty, respect, and authority are not gained only by being an expert. It can be gained by being vulnerable enough to ask subordinates to share their expertise and teach you. Everyone wants to feel they are needed and that they have something important to contribute. No matter how vulnerable you may feel, being open to receiving another's wisdom is like receiving a gift. Incorporating their ideas, knowledge, and opinions into decisions is like giving them a gift. It makes them feel they are instrumental in the big picture. They become invested in you. Your success is their success—a concept entirely contrary to the idea that people only follow leaders who have all the answers.

The second thing I learned was that, despite the challenges, I loved being in the armor branch and leading a platoon. My idea in college had been to get a chemical engineering degree that I could put to use in the civilian world after I'd paid back my four years to the Army because of my ROTC scholarship. Although I found chemical engineering interesting enough, I primarily thought it would be a lucrative field to go into with plenty of opportunities.

The point is, I wasn't planning to make the Army my career. But during those six months at Fort Hood, I caught a glimpse of a world that appealed to me—its aura, pride, camaraderie, and lineage. Being a leader in combat arms, especially armor, made me feel a part of something bigger than myself. The power of a tank grinding over rough terrain, the boom of its main gun, and the idea of being able to steer men through the exhilaration and terror of combat, spoke to me. At that time in history, World War II wasn't all that long ago, a war where tanks had ruled. And, even though the Vietnam War had largely been an infantry war, there'd been legendary armored outfits, such as the 11th Armored Cavalry Regiment, that boasted of awe-inspiring exploits and successes.

Armor felt a bit like a fraternity. The best part of college for me had been joining a fraternity. After a life of moving around, working to fit in, and trying to break into cliques that had already been long-established, my college fraternity was the first place I felt I belonged. I looked at combat arms similarly—it was a brotherhood in so many ways, and that spoke to me. Had I not been forced into a role I was not prepared for, forced to be vulnerable, I never would have found my calling, found the place where I belonged. I learned that sometimes willingly admitting your limitations can result in an unexpected bonus.

Having said that, it's not unusual for a young leader, like I was, to be forced into a situation where I had little choice but to admit my limitations and learn the ropes. But often, leaders don't understand the value of this. Instead, the whole goal seems to be to become knowledgeable as quickly as possible, so that asking for help or input is never required again. With that as the goal, the farther one climbs up the leadership hierarchy, the more likely the ability of high-ranking leaders to ask for input or help ossifies. Because decisions that are made at the highest levels usually have the greatest impact, this can become a real problem, as it was for the generals in World War I.

When I finished my six months as a tank platoon leader, I returned to my combat service-support branch and became a chemical platoon leader for nine months. After my brief taste of leadership in combat arms, being in charge of a service support platoon seemed dull and lackluster. I began to think that if I was going to be in the Army, I should be *in* the Army. And that meant a combat unit. Within a year, I transferred to the armor branch and soon found myself again in charge of a tank platoon at Fort Hood.

The first day I reported to my company commander, he told me my platoon was in the motor pool, where our tanks were being maintained. He suggested I should go down and introduce myself to them. On a blazing August day, I strolled into the motor pool, taking charge of my new job in a completely different way than I had previously. This time, I knew something about tanks. This time, I was part of the armor branch. In the heat, I could smell the welcome scents of hot metal and axle grease.

Our motor pool at Fort Hood could be typically found anywhere on Army bases: a two- to three-acre enclosed area that housed all the battalion's vehicles. It consisted of a limited-access, fenced-in, mammoth slab of concrete. A large building held numerous wide maintenance bays for repairing and servicing equipment. At the end of each day, all of the battalion's vehicles (tanks, jeeps, cargo trucks, and fuelers) were parked there—cleaned, topped off with fuel, and properly covered—in precision rows, all facing the same direction.

My new platoon sergeant was straddling the gun tube of his tank. He had just finished cleaning the bore evacuator—the bulge partway down a tank's gun barrel that removes gases and airborne residue after the gun is fired, so that they don't go into the turret of the tank. With a spanner wrench, he was tightening up the collar on the bore evacuator that held it in place.

No stranger now to tank maintenance, I strode up, wanting to impress him with my recently acquired knowledge.

"I'm Lieutenant Milano," I said. "Here, let me give you a hand." I reached up and grabbed the handle of the spanner wrench.

"No, don't . . ." he managed to get out before his middle finger, squeezed between the wrench and the gun tube, was shorn in two. The tip, about three-quarters of an inch in length, plopped onto the baking pavement.

With a cry of pain, he dropped to the ground, held his hand close to his chest, and writhed in pain. I pulled out the red handkerchief that all tankers carry and scooped up the piece of finger. I wrapped it gingerly and stuffed it into my pocket. Commandeering a Jeep, I took him to the battalion medical aid station, where he was immediately transported to the fort hospital. I accompanied him. All the way, he sat next to me, bent over, squirming with distress. Despite their best efforts, the doctors couldn't sew the tip back on.

I, of course, felt horrible, mortified. I prepared myself for the sure-to-come onslaught of, "What the hell were you thinking!?" questions from my leadership. Not an auspicious start to my burgeoning career as an armor officer. To his everlasting credit and character, my platoon sergeant never held that incident against me, and we ended up having an excellent working relationship for the few months before he moved on to another duty assignment. But, for me, the lesson was clear and one I never forgot: In any line of work, especially in a profession like the Army where dangers abound, hasty attempts to establish leadership credibility without the proper knowledge, training, and experience to back it up can have disastrous consequences.

The old adage, *a little knowledge is a dangerous thing*, was never more appropriate. My hubris and desire to be seen as the guy in charge resulted in unnecessary pain for my subordinate. And for no reason. This is the trap that awaits those who believe that leaders must know everything and who refuse to admit they have limitations. The paradox is that the more you do know, the more susceptible you are not to look for input from others—and the more likely you will make bad decisions based on the fallacy that you've arrived at being "large and in charge." To prevent this, at every step of the way up the ladder, leaders must work at remaining vulnerable leaders, in part by admitting their own limitations.

This takes practice on a regular basis. Seasoned leaders should periodically check whether they have fallen into the trap of no longer seeing their own limitations. They can do it by asking themselves these questions:

1. **When I ask a question, are people reluctant to answer?** When people think you want to hear only one thing, they will resist answering until they have a sense of what you're looking for.

2. **How many times do I ask for input from others in meetings?** If you are not looking for others' ideas or opinions, you might as well not have a meeting. You already know the answer.

3. **What is the motivation for my behavior? Am I doing this to further something, or am I doing it to be right or prove my brilliance?**

4. **Have I sought honest feedback from subordinates and peers about ways that I can improve my effectiveness? If yes, then what have I done with that feedback? If no, then why not?**

Although showing vulnerability by admitting limitations and seeking help from others can feel uncomfortable, result in unfavorable comparisons with others, and cause doubts about ability, these feelings will always be short-term. The benefits, on the other hand, will be long-term.

Years later, when I was a major and the new executive officer of a tank battalion at Fort Riley, Kansas, I ran into the sergeant whose hand I had mutilated. Apparently, he'd been in the battalion for a couple of years. He'd done well for himself and had been promoted twice since that incident ten years before. He was a first sergeant, the top noncommissioned officer in his tank company. Army-wide, only the best NCOs achieve such status. A meeting of the battalion's senior NCOs had just adjourned, and my battalion commander gave me an impromptu introduction. Standing there among the other first sergeants and the battalion command sergeant major, my former sergeant saw me and a big smile came across his face. He raised his hand, the middle finger a bit shorter than the rest, and said, "Hey, sir, good to see you."

I wonder if it was his way of giving me the finger.

‹ � ◆ ▸ ›

− 3 −

GETTING OUT OF YOUR COMFORT ZONE

*Vulnerability doesn't live
in your comfort zone*

Another way to practice vulnerable leadership is to look for opportunities outside of your comfort zone. *Merriam-Webster* defines comfort zone as *the level at which one functions with ease and familiarity.* Stepping outside a place of comfort automatically makes one vulnerable. It forces a person to be open to listening and learning. As we discussed in the last chapter, the goal of many leaders is to know all the answers so that they don't have to seek help or input; in other words, they want to reach a place of ease and familiarity and stay there. The problem with this is that it encourages complacency, a tendency to stagnate, and a lack of urgency. From within a comfort zone, a person focuses not on what needs to be done but only on maintaining the status quo.

Good leaders do the opposite. They continuously seek new opportunities that challenge both them and their team. They open themselves up to being vulnerable and strive to personally grow and develop. Stepping outside their comfort zones means they focus on forward momentum and a future vision rather than the past. Given today's rapidly changing, complex world, this type of leadership is more important than ever.

Even so, many leaders shy away from leaving their comfort zones. It is not difficult to understand the reasons why. Human beings naturally seek stability. They want to feel secure and content. They want to avoid risk and evade opening themselves up to painful possibilities. It is a universal instinct. When choosing to remain comfortable, the last thing a person considers is the cost of that decision.

When I graduated from high school, I had to find a way to pay for college at a good university. In New Jersey, where we lived, my father could afford to fund an education only at a public state school like Rutgers or Trenton State. Not that those schools weren't good, but I wanted something different. I sought an appointment through one of our senators to attend the United States Naval Academy at Annapolis, which was tuition-free. In fact, they'd pay me to go there. When I received the congressional appointment to attend the Academy, my father was pleased—thrilled, in fact—and I felt honored to be chosen.

Excited to learn what my next four years would be like, I visited Annapolis for a weekend and stayed with a friend I'd played basketball with in high school, Leo Latonick. He was a year ahead of me and had been recruited to the Naval Academy to play basketball. I stayed with Leo and his roommate and followed Leo around on both Saturday and Sunday. I observed his normal activities—formations, meals, physical training, and homework. He had no free time until late in the afternoons on both days. He showed me around the incredible facilities on campus and told me about the storied history of the place. I remember listening to music in his room on Saturday night but noted that drinking was off-limits.

He was pretty candid about his life at the Academy. They were required to stay on campus during the weekends—no trips home, road trips, or excursions into the city. He carried an intense academic load, and the amount of studying seemed a bit overwhelming to me. Schedules were highly regimented for everyone. It was a full-time commitment with only holidays and two weeks off in the summer. The rest of the year, they were confined to campus. At that time, the Academy was all male, with limited opportunities to socialize with women. Leo described his life at the Naval Academy almost with mild regret. His passion, basketball, was the thing that made it worthwhile for him.

Although I had enjoyed my visit, a sense of foreboding filled me on my way back home. Before the trip, I had assumed attending the Naval Academy would be a typical college experience, except I'd wear a uniform and have a few additional responsibilities. After spending time with Leo, it was clear it would be more than that. I would be signing up for a highly competitive, taxing, and demanding full-out engagement. It would require me to sacrifice hanging out with my friends and spending time with my girlfriend in New Jersey in exchange for an elite education. I wouldn't have basketball as an offset. I was a decent player but had no chance of making Annapolis's team.

A number of questions raced through my mind as I drove home. Could I go four years without seeing my girlfriend except during the short breaks allowed? Would she stick with me? Could I give up having summers off, partying with my friends, and being around women? Would I fit in? Would I be up to it? On top of all those concerns, the idea rattled me that, upon graduation as a newly commissioned Navy ensign, I would owe a minimum of five years of active-duty service. Doing the math, that meant I'd be 27 before I'd be free to do what I wanted.

Not long after the visit, I made up my mind not to accept the appointment. My father was incredulous, disappointed, and angry. No amount of cajoling or haranguing could change my mind, though. I received a couple of visits from an Academy grad my dad's age, who'd helped me secure my appointment, as well as a neighbor who'd gone there, both trying to convince me. All to no avail. I was firmly and unequivocally committed to staying within my comfort zone. Young, immature, and probably a bit insecure, I could see only the benefits of seeking a normal college experience, not the cost of turning down the exclusive opportunity the Academy offered.

In a huff, my dad told me I would have to pay for any school except a state one. I learned about the Army ROTC scholarship program from a high school counselor, and I decided that fit more neatly into my comfort zone. I could get a better education than at a state school, live a more normal college life, do ROTC, and have only a four-year active-duty commitment upon graduation. I was ready to slide comfortably into my next four years.

When I think back on my decision, while I avoided putting myself in a vulnerable position, I realize I missed out on an opportunity that would have challenged and pushed me. Perhaps even forced me to grow up sooner. Had I gone to Annapolis, I might have grasped why sacrificing my short-term wants for a greater good was important. Most definitely, I would have reaped the benefits of discipline. And maybe, I wouldn't have made some of the mistakes I did in my early adult years—marrying too young, not understanding my role as a husband, and getting divorced as a result.

Faced with another major career decision later in life, I chose differently. I opted for stepping out of my comfort zone.

When military officers progress in rank through their careers, the philosophy of "up or out" holds true. Being passed over for promotion to the next rank is a signal that the officer will soon need to leave the military, retire, or find a career in the civilian world. People can stay in the Army a few years after not being selected, but not long before confronting the inevitable. As an officer climbs in rank, fewer and fewer positions are available. Competition for the spots increases while the probability of snatching one of them decreases. Promotion rates drop significantly from major to lieutenant colonel and from lieutenant colonel to colonel, for example, until the promotion percentage from colonel to brigadier general is in the single digits. An increasingly narrow pyramid as one rises in rank turns into a needle. There simply isn't room for everyone.

In what the Army jokingly calls "Charm School"—a week-long course of instruction for newly selected general officers—the Army's Vice Chief of Staff told us to look around the auditorium and take stock of the other brand-new generals in the course. He paused and then added, "Realize that everyone sitting here can be replaced by any number of colonels who were not selected for promotion, and the Army won't lose a step." He went on to say that, by accepting promotion to general officer, each of us must acknowledge a stark reality. One day, the Army would say, "Thanks for your service—it's been great. It's time for you to retire." The cold, hard, but necessary, fact about Army life is that it is, and always will be, about the needs of the Army and not the individual.

When my time came to be given the goodbye handshake, I was a major general. I'd been led to believe I was on track for command of an operational division (where combat units are) since most of my experience rested there. Being given command of one was an extremely tough cut to make, though, with only 10 division commands in the active Army, a couple of which weren't suitable (airborne, for example). I didn't make that cut.

Instead, I was given two commands in the institutional Army, the first at Fort Knox, Kentucky, and the second at Fort Jackson, South Carolina. These installations conducted training activities such as basic combat training and professional military education to support the Army. While these commands were vitally important, upward progression from them was somewhat rare, and I could see the writing on the wall. I suspected the Army would bid me adieu at the conclusion of my two-year command at Fort Jackson. Even after having been fully warned in Charm School that this day would come, it still stung.

When I officially retired from the Army at the end of this last assignment, I wasn't ready to leave the workforce. For ex-Army officers, the natural transition into the civilian workforce is to go into the defense industry, which supports and supplies global military operations—companies like Lockheed-Martin, Raytheon, and General Dynamics. Many of these companies employ retired three- and four-star generals in their upper echelons who often recreate the Army culture within these civilian corporations. They routinely hire colonels and one- and two-star generals for many key assignments. Although these companies are part of the civilian world, their cultures are rooted in the military. The customs and courtesies of the Army, for example, calling a superior "sir," are alive and well. While stopping short of saluting one another, the hierarchical formality of the Army culture thrives. It makes for an easy transition to the private sector.

I was told by a retired four-star general, a mentor of mine, that I had a job waiting for me in Tucson at a large defense company as a vice president of something. Although I never went through the interviewing and hiring process, I assumed it wouldn't be too rigorous, much like the few interviews I'd had in my career in the Army. There'd been only three of them. One of them was when I was at the War College at Carlisle. My branch had nominated me and two others to contend for the G3 of a division that was deploying to Bosnia-Herzegovina in the summer of 1998.

I was flown in to interview with the division commanding general. I'd prepped and felt good about it. I walked into his office. We chatted for a few minutes and then he said, "OK, you've got the job. Now let's talk about getting this division ready to deploy . . ." It appeared he'd already made up his mind. I don't think he even interviewed the other two nominees. While not every interview in the Army was that easy, they generally weren't taxing. Considered a known quantity, a part of the club, I had no doubts that a job in the defense industry would be smooth sailing for me.

Remembering my decision about Annapolis long ago, I decided not to take that path.

Instead, I stepped out of my comfort zone and considered employment in the private sector within industries I knew little to nothing about and that were separate and distinct from the Army. By chance, during my second year of command of Fort Jackson, I met a long-time executive of Target Corporation at an event in Camden, South Carolina, where I delivered a speech as the guest of honor. He was a Senior Director, Distribution in the company and was apparently impressed enough to recommend me to his higher-ups.

Compared to my experience in the Army, the interview process for this job at Target was daunting. Once past the initial screening and a phone interview with the Executive Vice President for Global Supply Chain and Logistics, Target flew me to their headquarters in Minneapolis to interview in person. It turned out to be a three-day affair. On the first day, I was interviewed back-to-back by five two-person teams, all regional directors or vice presidents. All day long, behavioral questions were thrown at me. *Tell us about a time you failed to meet a deadline and what you did about it. Tell us about a project you led and how you motivated your team.* By the end of the day, I was exhausted.

On day two, I was sent to the distribution center in Minneapolis to spend half a day with its senior director, who happened to be an ex-Air Force guy. The facility was enormous—more than a million square feet—and clean as a hospital operating room. Everything in its proper place. The order, precision, neatness, and organization instantly appealed to my military mind. The senior director showed me around, introduced me to his team, and took me to lunch, all the while asking more questions and observing my reaction to the facility and the job.

I was impressed with how efficient the operation was and the level of engagement from everyone I met, from senior managers down to individual team members. A palpable, high-energy, can-do attitude emanated from everyone, a certain vibe that meant people were taken care of. After three decades of leading

Army units, the idea of leading a large, cohesive team spoke to me, and I could see myself fitting in. A distribution center was clearly a "field" operation, not part of the headquarters in Minneapolis, and that also made it attractive. I'd had a taste of navigating large, bureaucratic organizations in the Pentagon and hadn't cared for it. My interest in the job was more than kindled by the end of my visit, my mind overloaded with information.

From there, I flew to Cedar Falls, Iowa, to one of Target's food distribution centers, this one run by an ex-Army guy. It became clear it was no coincidence I'd been sent to these particular centers. Target wanted me to talk with other ex-military directors who'd made the same transition I would be required to make if I was offered the job. I was even more impressed with this facility and its operation and leadership.

The next step of the process came a few weeks later in a series of online leadership assessment exams and practicum sessions— about three hours each—that would be evaluated along with my interviews. Target was being thorough if nothing else.

About a month later on a Friday afternoon, I was driving to a meeting when my phone rang. It was Mitch Stover, the Executive Vice President for Global Supply Chain and Logistics and my potential new boss, a couple of echelons up. He offered me the job. When he told me the salary, I had to pull over. The offer was more than I'd made as a major general. But he cautioned that my onboarding journey wasn't over yet. I would be hired conditionally. I would have two months to shadow my predecessor, a month on my own, and then a final interview with the CEO. If the CEO was satisfied with me, the job would be mine. Mitch told me to think about it over the weekend and let him know.

I drove home on cloud nine. My wife, Kim, and I discussed our options, and on the following Monday, I accepted. I had taken a job I knew nothing about except how to lead.

During the three months before my final interview with the CEO, in addition to learning Target's business and figuring out my job and my team, I did everything I could to prepare. I diligently picked the brain of my predecessor as I shadowed him; I asked questions of my peers who'd gone through the process themselves. I researched the history of the company ad nauseam. I'd been told horror stories about interviews with the previous CEO—occasionally unpredictable and aggressive—and I didn't want to be let go so early in my new career.

As it turned out, I'd been overly concerned. Before meeting the CEO, I met with the Executive Vice President of Human Resources. Our interview went exceedingly well and paved the way for my discussion with the CEO. He was an avid sports fan, and our dialogue became more of a get-to-know-you kind of interview than a pass-through-the-gauntlet one. At least that was my impression. At any rate, after an almost four-month vetting process, I settled into my new job and began the next chapter of my life.

I can say that, during those four months, I was on the kind of high alert that leaving your comfort zone demands—in other words, completely vulnerable. All along the way, I scrambled to learn what I needed to navigate this new terrain. At times, my anxiety levels were sky-high. At times, I doubted myself. But I was also more open than I'd been in a long time. I felt excited, the way learning something new and interesting can light you up. Possibilities for the future were wide open. Not like in the Army, where the higher I rose, the more my future narrowed.

And although the interview process had been far more rigorous than in the Army, by the end of it, I felt that the effort and due diligence Target had done to assure they had chosen the right person for the job meant that I was valued as an individual. *Chosen.* Not just one of many general officers in Charm School that could be interchanged with one another. Had I not been willing to get out of my comfort zone, I never would have experienced that. I would have undoubtedly slid into a position in the defense industry. Just another interchangeable retired general officer.

I'm not saying that a person can't have a perfectly satisfactory life remaining in their comfort zone. The point I'm making is that excellence in anything, including leadership, can't be achieved without stepping outside of your comfort zone and allowing yourself to be vulnerable enough to make that leap. That is where growth and learning occur. I can honestly say that, when I left Target seven years later, of my own choosing, I was a much better leader than I had been in the Army—something that wouldn't have happened had I stayed in my comfort zone.

‹ ‹ ◆ › ›

-4-

ADAPTING TO DIFFERENT CULTURES

*Vulnerability can help close
the cultural divide*

Human beings are inherently social, which means we operate in groups. As anthropologist Ruth Benedict explained in her iconic book *Patterns of Culture*, "Society in its full sense . . . is never an entity separable from the individuals who compose it. No individual can arrive even at the threshold of his potentialities without a culture in which he participates."

And we participate in many different cultures—those of our country, town, family, race, religion, ethnic background, educational institution, membership group, and work, to name a few. Sometimes there aren't many differences among the social groups that make up our lives, and sometimes the differences are glaring. All of these groups, however, shape and influence our behaviors, sometimes in ways that catch us unaware. And each time we become a member of a new group, we bring our behaviors with us.

Every organization or corporation has its own distinct culture. Leadership behavior within these groups is strongly influenced by it. An extremely successful leader in one organization may fail dismally in another. Some leadership behaviors may prove advantageous in developing certain business partnerships, while the same behaviors may do the exact opposite in another arena.

It's always more comfortable to remain within one's own sphere. Unfamiliar cultures set off warning bells or beg to be ignored. An old African proverb sums up the situation best. "The stranger sees only what he knows." Faced with different cultures, there's a tendency to retreat to comfortable ground and rely on behaviors that have been successful in the past or to plow ahead blindly, oblivious to any differences at all.

I would argue that good leaders can succeed in any organization regardless of its culture, as long as they are willing to adapt. To do this, leaders must be vulnerable in the face of obvious differences and open to change. But first, they must acknowledge that not every culture *is* the same. Instead of blindly assuming the universe sees the world as they do, they must go into each new situation on the lookout for cultural clues. This is not always as easy as it seems.

So often in the corporate world when new management comes into an organization from the outside, they try to impose the culture they know on the one they've joined. After all, they've been brought in to fix a problem, and they believe if they duplicate what they did at their previous company, the results will be the same. Almost always, they fail to take into consideration that they have joined a distinctly different environment. When this happens, the results can be disappointing and painful. Leaders coming into a new organization would be wise to try to create change by working within the culture they've adopted, rather than trying to eradicate it.

Target, like many other retailers, knew it had to change its e-commerce business to compete against the new major online retailers. To help them revamp their business model, they brought in an executive vice president who had worked for 20 years at a global online retailing behemoth. He came from a culture that did not encourage leaders to be vulnerable. Instead, it encouraged them to make decisions quickly, trust their own opinions, criticize others unsparingly in the name of forward progress, and most importantly, get results. When this VP started at Target, he proceeded to lead in the same way he had at his previous employer.

It didn't go well. While his ideas were sound—Target needed to get out of its comfort zone and invest in new technology to deliver what its customers wanted—his execution fell short of its mark. He spoke to his subordinates and peers in a way that was very un-Target-like but completely acceptable at his previous company. He was oftentimes demeaning, arrogant, and insulting, and there was backlash. No matter how great his ideas might have been, people balked at his manner. His initiatives weren't wholly embraced.

It took him several months to realize that he would have to modify his behavior if he wanted to succeed. His tone changed. He started to listen and tried to understand the unique obstacles that Target faced in transforming to a new business model. He admitted that perhaps bringing leadership methods from his old employer wasn't working. Only by becoming a more vulnerable leader and working within the existing social constructs was he able to create the change he'd been hired to make.

When I was offered my job at Target, I knew I couldn't assume everything would be similar to the Army. Mitch Stover, the Executive VP who hired me, gave me some guidance. He told me that, while I was already a proven military leader, I was coming into a culture distinctly different, and I would have to modify my behavior. His message was clear—I needed to adapt to Target's culture or, no matter how good I thought I was, I'd fail. That was job number one. He told me that, in time, they'd teach me the business of retail logistics and distribution but that I would have to focus on Target's culture first. I took his input to heart. I went into my new position with my ears and eyes wide open.

At every turn, I could see I was, indeed, entering a different world. Where the Army had been directive, Target was more collaborative. In the Army, rank affected all interactions. There was a code of respectability, decorum, and social distance between the ranks that was strictly adhered to inside and outside of work. Every order given in the Army was followed, no questions asked unless it was illegal, immoral, or unethical. Not so at Target. While hierarchy did exist, orders weren't presented as imperatives. Instead, directives were made with the idea of winning people over, generating commitment, making a case convincingly, and persuading peers and subordinates it was the right thing to do.

When it came to managing people, the Army had been much more paternalistic. An officer was duty-bound to ensure the welfare of the people under his command. For example, if a soldier had an addiction problem, his commanding officer was responsible for getting him the help he needed. Not so in the corporate world. An employee with a drinking problem might be offered a help-line number to call, but not much beyond that.

Being overly involved in someone's personal life could even be considered crossing a line.

I noted these changes and adapted my behavior to match those around me. I prided myself on putting aside the trappings of my Army upbringing. I felt pretty good about my cultural metamorphosis.

About a month after I'd taken charge of my Target facility, at a morning update meeting, the Human Resources Manager asked if she could talk to me once the meeting broke up. She proceeded to skillfully point out that some of what I'd said in the meeting hadn't been useful and had, in fact, confused my team members. Her coaching took me by surprise. I was no stranger to leading briefing sessions. She explained that I used military jargon no one understood like telling my team we'd "aimed too low on the target" and that something was "high and right to me," among other things. Like calling meetings "briefing sessions." She said my stance and gestures could be considered off-putting and aggressive—hands on hips, arms crossed. My voice was loud and intimidating. All of it combined to make me less effective.

At that moment, it hit me that navigating cultural differences was much more nuanced than I had thought. It wasn't just following a different process or shifting the way I did something. It encompassed the words I spoke, the way I presented myself, the impression I gave, and the unspoken messages I sent. It cut closer to the core of my identity. It meant real change. If I wanted to fit into Target's culture, I would have to be truly vulnerable, take what the HR manager told me without offense, and pay more attention to the clues my team gave me. My behavior would have to change on many levels. Being vulnerable is realizing the impact you have on those around you and being aware of the impressions you make, sometimes without saying a word.

Would I have been a terrible leader if I had altered only *some* of my behaviors or even *none* of them? Probably not, but I wouldn't have been the best leader I could be. My leadership competency would have remained stuck in a past that was becoming less relevant.

Not only must leaders adapt to internal cultures like that of Target's, but they must also be sensitive to external ones. These include those of customers, suppliers, partners, and regulatory entities. In a global world, where business extends far beyond our borders, the array of external cultures has ballooned. The ability to adapt one's leadership behavior to work with or within many other cultures becomes paramount.

In 2007, I deployed to Iraq as part of a multi-national force after Saddam Hussein's regime toppled. I was a brigadier general, an assistant division commander, and one of my many responsibilities was to assist the Iraqi government—both national and local—in improving their country's essential services. These included water, sewage treatment, electricity, trash collection, and other public works projects. The conditions were miserable. During the first summer I was there, the citizens of the city of Baghdad could count on only an hour's worth of electricity each day. To make matters worse, Iranian-backed insurgents periodically shot holes in the transformers, causing the cooling oil inside to leak, which often resulted in the transformer overheating and exploding. And this was only one of the numerous problems facing the Iraqi people as they tried to grind out a daily existence with something resembling predictability.

I met each day with a wide variety of Iraqi officials and other U.S. national agencies like USAID to try to find practical solutions to improve conditions. Our goal was not to impose our way of life on the Iraqis but to provide our knowledge, resources, and assistance to empower them to become a self-sufficient democracy. In other words, we were supposed to provide the tools and training, and then go home. At least that was the plan. We were, after all, on their land and in their home.

To do this effectively, we had to understand not only the Iraqi culture but how to work within it. Before arriving in Iraq, we'd been briefed in detail on the country—its history of tribal factions like the Shia and Sunni, its major Islam religion, its traditional views toward women and the wearing of the *abaya* and the *hijab*, or head scarf, the prohibited use of alcohol, and more. But foreign cultures cannot be completely understood by reading about them; they must be experienced.

About six months into my assignment in Iraq, I was selected for promotion to major general. About that same time, General David Petraeus, who was the Commanding General of the Multi-National Forces—Iraq (MNF-I) tapped me to become the commanding general of the Civilian Police Assistance Training Team (CPATT), a position commensurate with my new rank. Although this meant extending my stay in Iraq by a year, I couldn't pass up the opportunity and, in reality, didn't have a choice in the matter.

As the Commanding General of CPATT, I was responsible for helping Iraq ensure the security of its society by training and equipping its 500,000-man police force (local, federal, river, customs, and facilities—anything Iraq had a police force associated with) and by making sure all were properly outfitted. The U.S. spent billions on police weapons, vehicles, forensic laboratories, equipment, and other resources to accomplish this goal. I also acted as the strategic advisor to the Iraqi Minister of the Interior, who oversaw his country's police and internal security apparatus.

One of the major foundations of any democracy is the establishment of the Rule of Law. This includes having a nonpartial justice system, a code of rights for the accused, an anti-corruption policy, a federal bureau of investigations, and forensics-based evidence, for starters. Little of this existed under Saddam's regime. For example, if a suicide bomb detonated in the street, the police and firefighters would rush to the scene and immediately hose down the area. Under our tutelage, they were trained to rope it off, treat it as a crime scene, and collect evidence.

Because the police force played a role in instituting the Rule of Law, I'd been asked to talk at a small luncheon in Baghdad. An FBI colleague in Iraq had invited me to speak about some of these issues and the approaches we were taking to address them. The luncheon was in the Green Zone, a controlled-access area in Baghdad where the Iraqi government was located, as well as our headquarters.

Baghdad is a complex city to navigate, with no street maps as we know them. An ancient city, its tiny streets and cluttered, compact neighborhoods are unlike anything we're accustomed to in the United States. As was typical, I wanted to be sure of the luncheon location. So, a couple of days beforehand, I sent my security team, consisting of British, Australian, and New Zealand security professionals, to scout out the event location. They arrived at a modest but well-kept home. Outside, a young Iraqi man was washing his car.

They got out and asked through a translator, "Is this where General Milano is supposed to be in a couple of days for lunch?"

The young man shrugged. "Sure, I suppose so."

The translator told my team, "Yes."

Two days later, we showed up at the same place around noon. Standing in the doorway of the house, a slightly overweight man dressed in an expensive but somewhat ill-fitting suit waited for us. I recognized him. He was a two-star general from the Iraq Ministry of Interior. (The Ministry of Interior had a rank structure similar to a military organization.) I'd seen him numerous times in my comings and goings, usually dressed in his uniform—navy-blue slacks and a short-sleeved shirt with major general shoulder insignia.

We'd showed up at what turned out to be his home (the young man washing the car a couple of days earlier was one of his sons). Politely but a bit stiffly, the general greeted us as we exited our vehicles. He invited us into his home. We sat down, and he served us chai tea. We made small talk, and it soon became apparent there'd been a major miscommunication.

Not only were we at the wrong place, but the general thought we were there to arrest him.

Under Saddam, corruption had been the way of doing business, which is why most government officials had been replaced. Perhaps the ministry official had taken part in it. Or perhaps he'd done nothing wrong. I imagined that when his son told him the CPATT commander had invited himself to lunch, the man could think of no reason for the visit other than being arrested, given a lifetime of authoritarian rule. For whatever reason, for two days, he'd prepared himself to be taken into custody. I was speechless. I had no intention of arresting anyone, nor had I any authority to do so.

As the misunderstanding dawned on our small team, a young man (likely an aide or assistant to our host), set food on a large dining room table adjacent to where we sat. The food had been prepared by the man's wife and daughters, who remained out of sight in the kitchen during our entire visit. I found it a bit disconcerting that, because of their culture, we were able to hear the women's voices but not see them. The food consisted of traditional Iraqi dishes—roasted lamb, chicken, rice, vegetables, *samoon* (homemade Iraqi bread), and fruit. Watching the young man lay out the spread, I realized the general expected us to stay for lunch. However, to make my speaking engagement at the FBI-sponsored luncheon, I would have to leave immediately.

While I assured the Iraqi general that we weren't going to haul him away, my aides unsuccessfully tried to contact the luncheon organizer to explain the situation. I stared at dish after dish being laid near us, their appetizing aromas permeating the room. Although there is nothing worse than being a no-show speaker, I realized I couldn't extricate myself from this man's generosity and custom of hospitality. In his culture, to turn down such an invitation would be an insult. I decided upsetting the FBI organizer was the lesser of two evils.

We stayed and enjoyed a delicious, albeit a bit uncomfortable, meal. Personal dignity, pride in home, and generous hospitality are a big part of Iraqi culture. If I ever needed proof of it, this bountiful lunch provided it. At a time when this man faced perhaps the most humiliating moment of his life, what had he done? Put on a suit, opened his home to his potential jailer, and entertained him lavishly. That idea would never cross an American's mind.

I could have left this man's house and made an appearance at my luncheon engagement. It turned out to be only a few minutes drive from the general's home. After all, he and his family had little to do with my job or mission. Instead, I learned an important lesson that day. There are bound to be misunderstandings when one culture collides with another. But when that happens, it is important that the misunderstanding is cleared up in a way that leaves both sides with their dignity. The only way to do this is to be vulnerable, admit your error, and honor whatever the other person requires from you. Handled this way, a mistake can provide deep insight into another culture. I can say I gained a greater respect for Iraq's culture that day.

In all business relationships, establishing trust is important. Without it, the possibility of doing business diminishes rapidly. Because different cultures view trust in different ways, it is important not only to know what trust looks like through someone else's eyes but also to be willing to forgo your own biases to establish that trust. And that requires being vulnerable enough to examine those cultural biases.

There's always an uneasy equilibrium when one country imposes itself on another. Even though the United States had sent troops to overthrow Saddam Hussein and help the Iraqis, we were still uninvited guests. It is safe to say that even the Iraqis who had not supported Saddam looked forward to the time when our presence wasn't a part of their everyday life. We were two different cultures, eying each other warily, a question of trust forever in the balance.

As the senior advisor to the Minister of Interior, Jawad Bolani, I spent a lot of time with him. Minister Bolani stood about six feet tall, a slim, balding man with salt-and-pepper hair on the sides and a neatly trimmed mustache. He'd been a colonel in the Iraqi air force during the Iran-Iraq war between 1980 and 1988. He smiled often, his dark, warm eyes lighting up his face.

He was gracious and amiable at all times. Behind his relaxed demeanor, though, was a sharp, attentive, and thoughtful mind. While he spoke some English, we communicated mostly through a translator.

Like many Iraqis in government and business, he rose late in the morning and ended his day in the wee hours of the morning. That was the norm. It wasn't unusual to have meetings with him at seven or eight in the evening after I'd already had dinner. Often, he'd insist I stay and eat with him. Not wanting to insult him, I politely forced down another meal that began and ended with chai tea, typically doused with sugar. Usually, he invited other Iraqis to join us, and we'd start our meal at nine or ten at night, sometimes not finishing until nearly midnight. I'd go back to my tin can of a room and sleep a few hours, rising in time to prepare for battle-update briefings that began at 6:30 in the morning. If Iraqis were night owls, Americans were early birds. Although my sleep suffered, I wouldn't have been able to do my job without accommodating my schedule to his.

A month into my role as Bolani's adviser, we flew to Washington, DC, so that he could meet with a host of high-ranking U.S. government officials. My job had been to prepare him for the meetings and make all the necessary arrangements. The afternoon we arrived, we checked into a hotel in Crystal City, near the Pentagon. He contacted me soon after and said he'd like to take a walk. I met him in the lobby, and we walked out into a sunny day.

A late afternoon in August, the air heavy with heat and humidity, the office buildings around us began to empty for the day. Still wearing his natty suit, he'd taken off his tie as an accommodation to the warm weather. We set out down the sidewalk, a few security personnel unobtrusively trailing us. We started talking about the upcoming meetings. Suddenly, he grabbed my hand in a friendly way and held it as we walked.

I stiffened immediately. Even though I knew it was a perfectly normal gesture in Arab culture, my first instinct was to pull my hand away. I hesitated. We were still getting accustomed to each other, and I feared I might insult him. Even so, his fingers wrapped around mine made me genuinely uncomfortable. Every fiber of my being was conscious of holding another man's hand on a crowded sidewalk in a bustling American city. *Even gay men in America are reluctant to hold hands in public*, I thought. Because even today, the sad truth is America does not openly accept public displays of affection for non-hetero pairings. And there we were in broad daylight, me dressed in slacks and a shirt, him in a tailored business suit, strolling along doing exactly that. I found it hard to concentrate on what he was saying, acutely aware of the fact that my hand was in his.

That is the thing about different cultures. A small gesture that carries so much weight and meaning for one culture can hold nothing for another. Minister Bolani walked placidly at my side, unruffled. Never had I felt more vulnerable or exposed. More concerned about what others might think of me. Part of me wished he'd worn Arab attire, a long loose gown called the *thawb*, with the flowing traditional headwear, to more clearly broadcast our differences—anything to alleviate my self-consciousness.

The walk lasted about 30 minutes.

I would like to say that after that experience, holding hands with men lost its significance for me, but that's not how things work. We are culturally programmed to react to certain behaviors, and until our culture changes, I suspect my first instinct will always be to pull back from another man's hand.

What did happen while holding hands during that walk was that trust and respect were established between Minister Bolani and me. My vulnerability that day allowed me to cross the cultural divide. I realized that he was signaling his friendship toward me by holding my hand. By accepting it, I did the same. And in all cultures, but especially Arab ones, friendship means trust.

The surest way to establish trust is to be vulnerable with another human being.

Walking down the streets of Washington, DC, minutes away from the Pentagon, that's exactly what we did. Minister Bolani and I put our trust in each other's hands.

‹ ‹ ◆ › ›

– 5 –

FACING THE FEAR OF
THE UNKNOWN

Fear makes us all vulnerable;
embracing it makes us powerful.

The expression *fear of the unknown* can cover a multitude of anxieties—fear of death, strangers, taking risks, making decisions, and even opening a door. What they have in common is *uncertainty*. No one knows what will happen when faced with the object of their fear. When someone takes a step into uncertainty, they immediately become vulnerable. Any of a number of consequences can play out—some positive, some negative, and some somewhere in between. The person is left exposed to these unknown factors. Everything is so unpredictable. No wonder people are anxious about putting themselves in such a vulnerable position.

However, our fears and reactions to them are, for the most part, internal. What may look frightening to one person may be less worrisome to another. While we can never eliminate uncertainty from our lives, we can learn how to effectively cope with the fear it produces.

This is an essential ingredient for strong leaders because their job often requires them to lead others into uncertainty. To show the way. To take the first step into the unknown. By showing vulnerability when faced with uncertainty, good leaders make it all right for those following to acknowledge their own fears. It provides an opening for discussion and results in a better plan for mitigating any potential obstacles ahead.

For this reason, good leaders must trust that being vulnerable will be beneficial, much as Minister Bolani and I trusted each other to hold hands in Washington, DC. This is not always an easy thing to master, because we are often our worst critics. All day long, the voice in our mind weighs in, passes harsh judgment, and interprets the external world in ways that are not always rational. We tell ourselves we'll be considered weak if we don't know something we believe we should. Or that by letting down our guard, others will see every flaw. In other words, we don't trust ourselves to be openly vulnerable. We are afraid of what might happen. This second-guessing ourselves further feeds our fear.

Until this internal judgment is quieted, openly facing fear is not possible. Success happens only when we have faith that we'll be up to the task of handling any outcome our vulnerability creates. True vulnerability begins, then, *within*. Without starting there, we're likely to avoid fear by not putting ourselves into a vulnerable position to begin with. We're likely to consign ourselves to a narrow corridor of already-tested ground, a place that doesn't produce forward momentum, innovation, or inspiration. In the words of writer Andre Gide, "Man cannot discover new oceans unless he has the courage to lose sight of the shore."

The good news is that the more leaders open themselves to vulnerability, the more comfortable it feels, and the more confident they become in mastering its outcomes. They learn that their worst fears are rarely realized. Evidence builds that they can manage uncertainty more effectively by being open and transparent about any doubts, fears, or reservations they harbor. They learn that vulnerability can actually make them better prepared for the problems that do crop up and allow them to find solutions more quickly.

Building this kind of confidence is part of the Army's individual training model for new soldiers entering basic combat training and for officer candidates seeking a commission. All are placed in situations where reliance on their team is fundamental to their success. For officer training, it's done through a series of exercises that force officer candidates to face their fears and trust their own capabilities. Only by doing so will they be able to lead by example and serve as an inspiration to their subordinates.

In the summer of 1978, I attended ROTC Advance Camp at Fort Bragg in North Carolina between my junior and senior years of college. ROTC Advance Camp, consisting of several thousand cadets from throughout the country, was a six-week program of physical and mental stress. I was in a platoon of 35 to 40 other officer cadet candidates, none of whom I knew beforehand. We were placed in various positions of leadership and challenged to lead our peers through a gamut of situations designed to teach us what small-unit leadership was all about. During the program, each cadet was assessed by the ROTC leadership who ran the camp. These assessments would be used to rank each of us at our respective colleges and universities, similar to how college athletes are ranked, and help determine what branch of service we entered. It was a challenging six weeks, easily the toughest thing I'd done in my life up to that point.

One of the required training events during Advance Camp was called the Slide for Life. This task required us to climb a rickety wooden tower about a hundred feet high onto a small platform, grab a T-bar hooked with a pulley onto a long, diagonally sloped steel cable, step off into thin air, and zip down the cable. At the signal of the ground guide, we had to let go over a pond of water, enter the water, and safely exit the pond. Simple enough.

Now, I will be honest. I am not a fan of heights. Throughout my entire life prior to this moment, I'd never jumped off anything higher than a stepladder. Not my idea of a good time.

Fear is not a rational thing. Intellectually, I knew the Army would not require me to do a training task that would hurt, maim, or kill me. The odds of me ending up injured on the Slide for Life were not great as long as I followed the instructions and training we'd been given. I witnessed with my own eyes the men and women ahead of me successfully completing the challenge. Even so, my mind screamed that I was headed for danger with a capital D.

I had no choice, though. Peer pressure is a persistent and effective motivator. My platoon mates ahead of me and behind me seemed to take the challenge in stride, at least outwardly, and I mimicked their behavior, despite my gut screaming otherwise. So, up the ramshackle tower steps I climbed, with a line of candidates following right behind me. I tried not to look down. It made me dizzy. My palms sweated. My heart thumped. My mind raced, searching for a plausible excuse to free me from going forward.

And then the T-bar was in my hands. Nowhere to go but down. I got the all-clear signal to step off. My feet stayed rooted to the spot at the edge of the platform. I could feel the guy behind me, waiting, and knew I couldn't delay any longer. I made myself focus on the task I'd been given. I stepped out. A rush of air, and I was swept away, moving at full speed, the water looming below me. At the signal of the person on the ground, I willed myself to let go with a terrified effort.

Cool water engulfed me. I had done it! I popped to the surface and looked up at the imposing tower I'd come from. My fear had made it seem a much greater distance. I clambered out of the pond, filled with more than relief. I'd never felt a greater sense of accomplishment.

Being able to act while in the grip of my fear of heights did, indeed, give me confidence. It also gave me the knowledge, forged by this experience, that fear needn't stop me. It became something more than an intellectual idea. I had bone-deep proof. It's hard to overstate my pride in overcoming such a strong fear.

I still have a healthy fear of heights, but what I gained that day by trusting myself to act in the face of it makes it less of an issue. Many years later, when I was in Iraq, my job of advising the senior officials of Iraq's Ministry of Interior brought me to confront my fear of heights again. The building that housed the Ministry of Interior was one of the tallest buildings in Baghdad, fifteen stories high. One of the major generals in charge of the Ministry's Internal Affairs, with whom I regularly met, had his offices on the top floor. Because the elevator that serviced the building was unreliable and frequently stalled, we never took it. Instead, we hiked up fifteen flights of stairs. It was tough— packing roughly 40 pounds of body armor, carrying weapons, and wearing our helmets. All in stifling heat. Although the building was spottily air conditioned, the stairwell had none. By the time I, my translator, security detail, and whatever expert was accompanying me reached the top floor, we were sucking air and sweating profusely.

Thankfully, the Iraqi general's office was air-conditioned. He usually shared information about the corruption investigations he was conducting, followed by lunch. We ate on a small glass-enclosed balcony, just off his main office, with a breathtaking view of Baghdad and the surrounding areas on all three sides. We could see for miles when the haze wasn't bad. The balcony literally jutted out from the building, suspended in air, with nothing below but space. (My palms are growing damp just writing this). Needless to say, it was a bit harrowing. I had the urge to hug the floor. Knowing that the Iraqi construction codes were not nearly as rigorous as those in the United States added to my unease.

But, remembering my Slide for Life experience, I knew I could make myself sit on that gravity-defying balcony and finish my meal, despite heart palpitations calling out dire warnings. I could almost enjoy the delicious meal—lamb, chicken, rice, and vegetables served in the traditional Iraqi style. I made myself focus on the task at hand and avoided looking away from the table, especially not directly downward. And while I can't say these luncheon meetings on a dangling balcony changed my preference to remain tethered to the earth, I was able to function normally every afternoon I spent there.

Being present with my fear made me vulnerable to myself. I listened empathetically to my mind's concerns and criticisms and didn't judge. Doing that diminished my fear. This is the power of being vulnerable, not just to the outside world but also to yourself, of not letting the critic in your mind get the upper hand. And acknowledging and confronting my fear made me more empathetic to others who, despite outward appearances, might be struggling with their own internal fears.

The Army is full of paradoxes. On one hand, it doesn't encourage what I call *personal vulnerability*—when a leader admits they don't have total command over their individual circumstances. There is an expression used half-jokingly in the Army, "Sounds like a personal problem to me." Leaders often say this in situations when something doesn't go as planned because an individual doesn't appear to have control of some aspect of his life, when a personal issue interferes or impacts someone's ability to do a job, or even when a person is simply late. Essentially, it means, *I really don't care about your personal circumstances. They're your problems, and you need to sort them out. We have a mission to do, so get your shit together and accomplish your tasks.*

Although not everyone necessarily feels or believes this in the Army, the expression exemplifies a culture that expects there to be no chinks in certain aspects of a soldier's life. There are Army programs to help with major issues in life like financial problems or alcohol abuse. But other personal matters that can impact performance—marital issues, anxiety, depression, or having reliable transportation, for example—are expected to be handled. While the Army is trying to change this, the fact remains that the culture has been an environment where participants don't feel free to discuss personal challenges, anxieties, or ignorance.

On the other hand, the Army does do a good job of forcing its officers to continually face the unknown in their jobs. Almost every couple of years, an officer changes jobs, often due to promotion or career-enhancing opportunities. No sooner have they conquered the ins and outs of one job than they are moved to another one that has greater responsibilities that they know little about. This is what I label *situational vulnerability*. Being thrust into a new position, often with increased responsibility and scope, creates both a fear of the unknown and built-in vulnerability.

Every time it happened to me in the Army, I felt apprehensive, unsure of my knowledge, and unclear about how to be effective in my new job. A few weeks into most jobs, I typically experienced uncertainty and inadequacy, especially in those positions where the learning curve was steep—as in the Pentagon, for example. Sure, I'd seen others do the same job, and I'd filed away behaviors that I liked and things I didn't, but until I was in the saddle, it hadn't been real. Years later, when I talked to fellow officers, I found they'd all had similar experiences. Those of us who handled the challenge by embracing this enforced vulnerability seemed to fare better than those who didn't.

When assigned to a new position, there's usually a brief period of overlap when the outgoing commander or staff officer hands the job off to the new one. Some leaders are better at orienting their replacements than others. Some keep no secrets, freely share areas of concern, and recommend areas of focus for the incoming person. They realize it's in everybody's best interest for the next commander to also succeed. Others can be more guarded, unorganized, and almost resentful that the Army is moving them on to something else. They do the minimum amount to help their successor. I experienced examples of both types of leaders several times in my career.

In June of 1990, while I was part of the 11th Armored Cavalry Regiment stationed in Germany, I witnessed the latter approach firsthand. The outgoing commander treated the incoming one begrudgingly. He didn't share much and gave the impression that he didn't have time for the new commander. They had widely different styles—the incoming commander led both by example and with his intellect (he'd written extensively on professional topics, including an excellent history book about the Army in the 1950s), and the outgoing commander led more by action. When I showed the outgoing commander the program for the regimental change-of-command ceremony that included the two men's professional bios, he grunted, "Huh, I guess some guys write about it and some guys do it."

The reality was that the incoming commander, despite his intellectual tendencies, was eminently qualified to assume command. In this dance of handing over authority, there is opportunity for vulnerability on both sides of the transaction. Thankfully, the incoming commander took it in stride, confident he'd figure it out. And he did.

The best commanders I observed coming into a new position were smart; they issued no new policies, made no major changes, moved no personnel, and did nothing of significance for at least 30 days. They simply observed, gathered information, talked to people, and saw for themselves the workings of the organization and people before making changes. They remained in a vulnerable no-man's land and resisted any pressure to act quickly. They freely admitted they didn't have all the answers and relied on others to help set them up for success. I used this same model to great effect in the organizations I was fortunate to lead.

I've also seen new commanders come in and immediately change everything—personnel, policies, routines. Nothing demonstrates a lack of vulnerability more. Although rarely openly stated, the message the commander gives in this approach is that *things are so screwed up, I need to make drastic changes. Thank goodness I'm here to right the ship.* The price of having to demonstratively show they have all the answers is that commanders like this succeed only in conveying a low regard for the outfit they've taken over.

When I became the Director of Training for the Army in 2005, I tried to follow the method used by the best commanders. I was a new brigadier general, and, although I'd previously served at the Pentagon, it had been with the Joint Chiefs of Staff and not with the Army Staff. The Army Staff was a culture unto itself—one that prided itself on working hard and spending more time on the job in the Pentagon than the other service staffs (Air Force, Navy, Marines). It was a culture of grind—working 12 to 15 hours a day and most Saturdays. In fact, their motto was: *There are those who work 12-hour days or longer . . . and then there are those who proudly work a habitual pattern of even longer hours.* Not many enjoyed their time at the Pentagon, but it was a rite of passage most officers had to perform at some point in their careers.

So, with some trepidation, I embarked on my new job as the Director of Training, fresh from a year-long deployment in Kuwait. I was responsible for all policies, programs, and budgeting related to training, developing the Army's training strategy, and managing 130 different training programs. These programs covered the full spectrum, from individual to large-scale combat training. They covered not only live training but also virtual and constructive training for active duty, National Guard, and Reserve Component troops. It included making sure units were trained and ready to deploy, that all soldier, NCO, and officer professional-development programs were executed, and that enough ammunition was on hand and in the pipeline for both training exercises and going to war.

Perhaps most critical of all, I was responsible for the budget that would support all this activity. In other words, it was a lot of responsibility. I had a team of about 50 people—officers, NCOs, and civilians—to help me make it happen, including my right-hand man, the Deputy Director of Training, who'd been in his role for years. With little knowledge about how this part of the Pentagon worked, I stared deeply into the unknown.

I soon found out that, to thrive in that place, I had to overcome bureaucratic hurdles at every turn. No matter how minor the task, there was always some person who had to be consulted before it could move forward. Finding that person became an exercise in coordination and discovery, much like threading a path through a maze. I took a deep breath and tried to emulate those officers I'd watched successfully navigate this ritual of being tossed into unfamiliar territory. I watched, listened, asked questions, and didn't rush into major decisions.

Many of my staff were civilians who had been on the job at the Pentagon for years and understood this bureaucratic morass like a well-traveled map. I was completely reliant on them, as well as on my Deputy Director of Training and my principal subordinates. It was very clear to me how integral they were to the success of our directorate. Instead of bluffing my way through or pretending to have all the answers, I deferred to their expertise.

Perhaps the biggest challenge I faced was effectively handling the budgeting process. The five-year training budget was updated every year in a continuous process. The training desires and needs of the entire Army were funneled up through the Army hierarchy to me on the Army Staff. From there, we determined the overall training requirements and vetted each of the 130 requested programs. They were then fit into our overarching strategy to ensure the Army's priorities were being addressed. At the time, we were at war in both Iraq and Afghanistan, so we had to make sure our training support enabled the Army to function properly in those wartime conditions, and that individuals and units were at the highest possible readiness before deployment.

After going through this complicated process for the next five-year increment, we determined we had $21 billion worth of requirements. We sent the requested budget to the people on the Army Staff—the Program, Analysis, and Evaluation (PA&E) directorate—who validated it. They ranked and stacked our training requirements against the Army's total needs (things like force modernization, new-equipment funding, supporting war efforts, and personnel costs). When it came back from PA&E, they had validated only $17 billion of our training requests. Then, the budget folks who actually allocated the money told us we'd be funded at $14 billion, citing other bills that had to be paid and other priorities. I ended up with only two-thirds of what had been requested—$7 billion short.

My job wasn't over. My team was faced with the prospect of going back to all the areas in the Army that had requested funding and allocating this $7 billion shortage across their 130 programs. Of course, no one is ever happy to have their budget cut, but we had no choice. The money wasn't there. Plus, in accordance with Army priorities, some programs received little to no shortfalls, while others took big cuts. It was all about priorities.

There was more jockeying and negotiating. Sometimes, the cuts were reluctantly accepted, and, at other times, it was a battle, like with the Superintendent of West Point. He felt that, since he represented the United States Military Academy, they should be spared cuts (I was professional but unsympathetic, being a product of our ROTC program). I told him politely that I disagreed. Mind you, he was simply doing what he was supposed to do—advocate for his particular need. He took his complaint to my boss, who told him to buck up and take the shortfall. A contentious time, and I had no previous experience in having to sell and defend my decisions to the entire Army in a very political environment. I would have embarrassed myself if it had not been for my team and others who helped.

As it was, I felt like I'd fallen short. I had managed to secure only two-thirds of the budget for the Army's training needs. In my mind, I deserved a failing grade. My staff brushed off my concern as if it was all in a day's work. And although it was hard for me to equate what I thought were dismal results with success, I put my faith in them that we'd done all we could.

When I met with my boss at the end of the year, I prepared myself for a less-than-satisfactory efficiency report (performance evaluation), but my boss told me that his boss, the Chief of Staff of the Army and in charge overall, thought I'd done a good job and that he'd like to keep me on as the Director of Training for another year. He affirmed what my staff had been telling me all along. My stint as the Director of Training had been a success, no matter what the critic in my mind was saying.

I realized I had fallen into another trap. Often, when we take a step into the unknown, we continue to measure our performance the way we have in the past. We don't take into consideration that the metrics have changed with our new circumstances. With one hundred percent always being my goal, seventy percent seemed a failure. But when we use an outdated yardstick, we can't assess the situation properly, and it can easily become a vicious circle. The more inadequate we feel, the less likely we are to allow ourselves to be vulnerable the next time, which means we are less likely to adapt our behavior to what's required.

As we go through our careers and lives, we can't avoid facing fear and uncertainty, especially if we want to progress. When staring down the unknown and our fear of it, we have two choices. We can recoil in discomfort and cling to what we know, or we can become vulnerable enough to take a step forward and be open to whatever comes next.

I've mentioned three different types of vulnerability: *self, personal,* and *situational vulnerability.* Often, it may seem that we have no choice about being vulnerable—the critical voice in our mind takes control, our personal circumstances demand attention, or we are forced into a situation not of our making. What matters, however, is how we approach and handle each of these inevitable parts of life.

If our mindset is one of what I call *intentional vulnerability,* we can work with whatever fear grips us. *Merriam-Webster* defines the word "intentional" as "done by intention or design." Inherent in this definition is choice.

So, the next time you are faced with uncertainty or fear of the unknown, choose the path of vulnerability. Choose to give the critic in your mind a polite *No, thank you.* Choose to be open and honest with yourself and others. Choose to ask for help. By doing that, looming fears or obstacles will shrink and make your task infinitely more manageable.

‹ ‹ ◆ › ›

-6-

LEARNING GOOD LEADERSHIP
BY STUDYING OTHERS

*Vulnerability requires
a will to learn*

When you mention the word "learning," most people think about school and formal education. But learning isn't a rote memorization of facts regurgitated at test time. Rather, it is the innate process in human beings that allows them to gain knowledge. Behavioral psychologists have a theory to describe this process, called "social learning." It goes like this. When a person encounters new information, the first item of business is to observe the thing in action, along with its context. Then they compare it to what they already know and decide how it fits into their lexicon of knowledge. Finally, they store the information in their memory and apply it in their own life.

This makes sense. No one learns how to play baseball by sitting all alone at their desk and reading an instruction manual or memorizing statistics. Instead, people observe other people demonstrating the game, compare it to other games they know, store the rules and physical motions in their memory, and then participate in an actual game. To learn the intricacies and strategies of baseball and become a better player, this process is repeated over and over again to fine-tune and internalize any refinements.

This is how we learn the most important and basic things in life. For example, following a recipe would be impossible without understanding the basic concepts of cooking—what a stove is and how to use it, what purpose kitchen utensils serve, and what measurement means. We usually learn these things not from a cookbook but from watching other people demonstrate them for us in the kitchen. That's why behaviorists call it "social" learning. We learn from others who share their experience with us.

We also learn how *not* to do things by observing others and incorporating the lesson into our personal book of knowledge. A child hits another child at school, and the rest of the class observes what happens. Those observing the consequences of this bad behavior don't have to do the act themselves to learn that hitting isn't an appropriate behavior. They make the connection, file it away in their memory, and then refrain from behaving similarly to avoid being ostracized, having privileges taken away, or experiencing the other repercussions the incident caused.

While these are simple examples of social learning, most of our behavior is shaped in this manner—everything from how to tie our shoes to how to behave at a formal dinner.

Leadership is a sophisticated form of social behavior. There is no leadership manual with a set of instructions that can churn out competent, effective leaders. Certainly, there are plenty of leadership books that talk about the subject and offer guidelines. But no matter how many of these books a person reads, they will still have to learn what good leadership means by studying others doing it well or poorly—or both. Leadership behavior must be observed, internally vetted, and incorporated into how we act.

The question then becomes, *Why are there so many examples of poor leaders in the world?* Why don't people just observe the best leaders and emulate them? After all, no one ever models themselves after lousy baseball players; everyone tries to play like Babe Ruth, Derek Jeter, or Aaron Judge. As Douglas Adams, author of *A Hitchhiker's Guide to the Galaxy*, mused, "Human beings, who are almost unique in having the ability to learn from the experience of others, are also remarkable for their apparent disinclination to do so."

Personally, I think there are two reasons why more leaders aren't studying the best and worst leaders to improve their own leadership skills. First, they don't recognize who these people are. The definition of "good leadership" is not always clear or agreed upon. Second, for a variety of reasons, many leaders don't believe other people's experience is of value. They believe their situation is unique and hasn't been experienced before—and that, therefore, no one else has anything useful to share.

Let's examine the first reason why studying good leaders is problematic. What exactly are the behaviors that make someone a great leader? The U.S. Marine Corps has 14 traits it believes make leaders most effective: *Bearing, Courage, Decisiveness, Dependability, Endurance, Enthusiasm, Initiative, Integrity, Judgment, Justice, Knowledge, Loyalty, Tact,* and *Unselfishness.* Sounds like a good list, doesn't it? But in researching what others think are the most important traits of good leadership, I found no consistency. Everybody's top 10 differed. Here is a compilation of just some of the additional traits/behaviors that various "experts" believed were key:

Accountability	Adaptability	Ability to inspire	Awareness	Ability to Influence
Balance	Benefit of the Doubt	Being Considerate	Bottom-line focus	Cooperation
Commitment	Credibility	Collaboration	Citizenship	Civility
Congruence	Confidence	Conflict resolver	Charisma	Creativity
Decisiveness	Empowerment	Empathy	Effective Communicator	Focus
Forgiveness	Gratitude	Going above and beyond	Humility	Honesty
Intuition	Innovation	Kindness	Listening	Motivator
Master Delegator	Optimism	Positivity	Patience	Pleasing Personality
Recognition of Others	Respectfulness	Self-control	Sympathy	Self-awareness
Risk-taker	Stability	Strategy-minded	Teacher	Transparency
Time Management	Team-builder	Understanding	Visionary	Vulnerability

Although this is by no means an exhaustive list, it doesn't matter. Any list of traits does little to define or illuminate the essence of a good leader—because it doesn't show us how embodying these traits translates into good leadership behavior. Only by seeing these traits and their consequences in action can we understand what good leadership looks like. The list also doesn't answer the question of which traits are critical and which are nice to have—or if different behaviors are more important than others in certain circumstances. For example, empathy may not be a top contender for the Marines, but should it be key for someone in the mental-healthcare industry or a charitable organization?

Equally difficult is the definition of poor leaders. Let's assume their traits and behaviors are the opposite of those listed above. Easy enough, right? In reality, most humans have neither all positive nor all negative traits, but a combination of both.

Historically, many bad leaders had initiative, creativity, loyalty, and charisma. They were risk-takers and results-driven. They were greatly admired by some people and lauded in the press. In the 1920s, students at the Medhill School of Journalism at Northwestern University listed the gangster Al Capone as one of the 10 outstanding personages of the world. True, he embodied some of the traits above—he was decisive, collaborative, focused, and confident—but he was also ruthless, greedy, egotistical, and lawbreaking. And then, there was the small matter of murdering people.

Today, many of our business and political leaders no longer exhibit moral integrity or civility, and yet they are considered successful and admirable by some.

Is the definition of good leadership determined, then, by societal opinion? If so, in America today, it seems being successful is the only criterion needed to be considered a good leader (having wealth may be a close second). By being successful, I mean that a person has met or exceeded whatever performance metrics are set for the work they're doing. They double their profits every year or expand their business into every state, for example. This becomes such a broad definition that anyone with subordinates who consistently meets goals could be considered a potential role model. History tells us, though, that simply achieving desired results doesn't necessarily make a leader exceptional or particularly effective in the long run.

Jack Welch, a former Chief Executive Officer (CEO) of General Electric Corporation (GE), was considered the best manager of the 20th century for decades. During his reign at GE and for many years after, he was held up as the gold standard for CEOs. He took over the company in 1980 and proceeded to make radical changes to an, arguably, already-successful company. His goal was to make GE one of the most valuable companies in the world. By "valuable," he meant that it provided its shareholders with consistent and generous returns each quarter.

He was wildly successful. GE shareholders and Wall Street were ecstatic. He accomplished his goal by cutting the fat and downsizing his company, firing the bottom-performing 10% of his workforce each year, divesting any businesses that weren't in the number one or two spots in their industry, and exploiting loopholes in regulations governing corporate finance. He became a superstar CEO, bottom-line driven, with a take-no-prisoners approach.

Other company leaders mimicked his leadership style. Many of his protégés went on to run major corporations like Home Depot, Chrysler, and Honeywell, taking his methods with them. Numerous books and articles were written about his success, and consulting firms helped their clients integrate his approach into their organizations—all of which would suggest that Jack Welch was a leader worth studying and emulating.

In May of 2022, David Gelles' book about Jack Welch, *The Man Who Broke Capitalism*, hit the bookshelves. In an interview, Gelles said, "Jack is the apotheosis of everything that is wrong with capitalism over the last 50 years." In Gelles' measured view, instead of the leadership standard of the 20th century, Welch was a disaster for capitalism. He traced many of the problems we face in our corporations today to Jack Welch's leadership legacy—excessive executive pay packages, lack of concern for employee welfare, an unengaged workforce, lack of long-term focus due to chasing short-term shareholder gains, a dearth of innovation, and celebrity CEO worship (think Elon Musk).

Although Jack Welch was successful in the short term, GE did not fare well after he left and probably will never recover its former glory. Some of his protégés who went on to run other companies failed spectacularly as well. For example, Bob Nardelli, a former GE executive, was named one of CNBC's worst CEOs of all time. He was fired by Home Depot because he alienated his executives, refused to cut his outrageous pay package, devalued customer service, and lost market share.

While Jack Welch had many of the qualities that are attached to good leaders, he made the mistake of defining success too narrowly and adhering to it too rigidly. Performance was based largely on meeting budgets and financial goals tied to shareholder returns. Not hitting these goals meant the possibility of employees landing in the bottom 10% and losing their jobs. That's a recipe for a cutthroat environment that doesn't encourage trust, teamwork, or honesty. Putting so much attention on meeting short-term profits also discouraged risk-taking and longer-term innovation. Without those, there isn't much chance of coming up with the next best thing. Although Welch talked about values and the importance of people in his organization, the message he sent was that neither was a priority.

This is the problem with defining good leadership as simply achieving results. How those results are achieved makes a difference. Leading requires the ability to get results through others and having an eye on the long-term future. Achieving quarter-by-quarter results is not sustainable without an investment in the workforce and adapting to changes in the marketplace. Any definition of "good leadership" must consider these crucial areas as well.

So simply emulating a successful leader does not make someone a great one, as many of Welch's disciples showed.

Contrast Jack Welch with Target's CEO, Brian Cornell. He began his career in retail right out of college and worked his way up the corporate ladder. Before coming to Target, he did stints as CEO at Sam's Club and Michaels and was being groomed as the likely replacement for the then-CEO of Pepsi.

On December 19, 2013, Target discovered that it had suffered a massive data breach—one of the largest in history. During Black Friday, hackers stole information from 40 million credit and debit cards as well as from 70 million customer records. Although Target managed the breach as well as could be expected, the damage was crippling. Consumers lost trust, and earnings fell 46% following the holidays. Twenty-seven states filed claims against Target, and the company settled them for $18 million. Altogether, the breach cost the company more than $200 million. The CEO at the time, Greg Steinhafel, resigned.

With the company still in a tailspin from the breach, Brian Cornell took over the helm. At the time, like most retailers, Target was losing market share to Amazon, which had upset the whole retail paradigm. The outlook for Target was gloomy. When Brian took over, I'd been with the company for more than two years. Given the state of the business, a lot of us braced ourselves for the "New Guy Syndrome"—a hotshot coming in from outside and immediately reorganizing, letting people go, and imposing what had worked for him in other companies on Target's culture.

But Cornell didn't do that. Then in his fifties and unassuming, he spent much of his early days on the road, visiting stores and distribution centers (including mine)—even talking to customers—and getting the lay of the land.

He freely shared his own challenges during his upbringing. His mother suffered from heart disease and survived on welfare, so his grandparents brought him up. He worked his way through UCLA, taking whatever jobs he could, including washing Tropicana trucks in New York City. He was proud of being so self-reliant, and grateful for what he'd achieved.

To my surprise, he was one of the best listeners I've ever met among senior leaders. As we spoke, I genuinely felt he wanted to hear what I had to say. He listened in a manner that was sincere, respectful, and engaging. He struck me as a down-to-earth, decent person, certainly not some hotshot with all the answers. After gathering data firsthand, he developed a strategy to move Target forward. The plan was future-oriented, designed to increase Target's competitiveness, reinvigorate its brand, leverage its reputation, and, ultimately, provide guests with multichannel options for how they wanted to shop.

His plan couldn't be implemented overnight. I recall vividly a CNBC interview with him in 2016. As part of his plan, he convinced the board to spend $10 billion to improve

Target's woefully inadequate e-commerce platform. Without it, Target stood no chance of being competitive against Amazon's juggernaut.

His interviewer, blond and perfectly coifed, listened with a smirk on her face as he explained the investment and how it would be used.

"Ten billion dollars in your e-commerce platform? Really?" she chuckled. "How much longer do you think you're going to have your job?" she asked, implying what many people thought.

He gave her a brief smile and gracefully explained—again—the logic of what he was doing and why.

And it proved to be a brilliant move. He brought in experts and surrounded himself with great talent to help drive improvements in all facets of the business. Target's e-commerce business grew, and the company's stock is valued at three times what it was then. He also brought a strong commitment to team-member engagement, inclusivity, diversity, and leader development. Under his leadership, the results of Target's annual Best Team Survey (measuring employee engagement) were serious business. Although the survey had been around for a while, he brought a greater rigor to it, personally wanting to know what his leaders were doing with its results.

Like Welch, he increased shareholder value, maybe not as consistently or generously, but he did it with the company's brand and its employees' well-being in mind.

In 2017, during our annual sales meeting of store and distribution leaders, Target did a salute-to-veterans' campaign. Brian led a panel of five former military service members, which included me. We sat on a platform in front of a few hundred Target leaders. Brian led the discussion, asking questions, commenting on our careers, and picking out the leadership points he wanted to amplify. He did a masterful job.

Afterward, he pulled me aside and talked to me for about 15 minutes. He wanted to know what it was like being a general in combat, leading soldiers. I was the first former active-duty general to work for Target, and he wanted to understand the leadership challenges I had faced. He pelted me with questions: What were my days and nights like? How'd my family deal with my deployments? What were some things I was particularly proud of? What were the toughest decisions I faced? What did I think corporate leaders could learn from the Army? I couldn't help thinking, *Here was a man in the top spot, still interested in learning about leadership from others.*

I don't think we can all agree on how to define a good leader. But I hope I've convinced you that simply being successful is not enough. A leader must be effective not only in getting results but by doing it through others in a way that is sustainable and leaves the organization viable in the future. And yes, many of the things listed earlier—listening, vulnerability, commitment, empowerment—are necessary. But merely talking about them or possessing them doesn't automatically make someone a good leader. They must be put to use in a way that creates not only success but also a successful environment for *everyone*, as Brian did at Target.

Throughout history, we've had a lot of leaders who've shown this kind of leadership and should be studied, but are not. As mentioned previously, many people believe that past experience is not relevant to today's situation or them personally. And they're partially right. Technology, social norms, and new innovations do make some things in the past irrelevant. But leadership is not one of them. As long as humankind has been a social species, leadership has been in play. Even if the tools or norms or circumstances have changed, the requirements of leadership have not.

But fear of irrelevance isn't the only thing that gets in the way of us learning from others and history. As the writer Samuel Taylor Coleridge said, "If men could learn from history, what lessons it might teach us! But passion and party blind our eyes, and the light which experience gives us is a lantern on the stern which shines only on the waves behind us."

Unfortunately, this phenomenon has been true of some of our military leaders. Even though the tools of war have changed over the years, the leadership challenges remain the same. That is why, in many of the Army's officer-leadership schools, leaders of the past are studied and considered still relevant. Take, for example, the two leaders in the battle of Gettysburg during the Civil War.

General George Meade took over as commander of the Union Army of the Potomac a couple of days before the battle of Gettysburg. He was asleep in his tent when a messenger roused him early in the morning hours of June 28, 1863. Groggy, he assumed he was being relieved of command, given the Union defeats at recent battles. On the contrary, the messenger had come from President Lincoln, who was promoting Meade immediately to the commander of the Army of the Potomac. Meade replaced General Joseph Hooker, who had been in command for roughly six months and had recently lost decisively to General Robert E. Lee at Chancellorsville in early May of that year.

New to his position, Meade quickly had to learn the disposition of his Army and figure out how to defeat General Lee and his Army of Northern Virginia which threatened from the north. Meade had little time to get up to speed. Lee's invasion into Pennsylvania posed a significant threat to the Union. Meade arrived at Gettysburg late during the night of July 1st, the first day of the three-day-long battle.

He gathered his subordinate commanders together, and rather than dictate from his position of authority, he solicited their advice on tactics the Army might use to defeat Lee. He realized he needed their experience, insight, and recommendations. He actively sought their opinions in an open forum, reserving judgment until he'd heard them out. Some advocated maneuvering to more defensible terrain, some urged Meade to stay and fight on the ground they currently occupied, and others advocated attacking Lee offensively. His ultimate decision was to stay and defend the ground they occupied south and east of the town of Gettysburg. It proved to be a successful strategy and led to victory over Lee in battle.

On the other hand, Lee's leadership style was the exact opposite. Although well-liked—even revered—by his men, Lee dismissed the input of his subordinate commanders. His most trusted commander, James Longstreet, strongly urged Lee not to attack the Union army, to maneuver to more defensible terrain, and to force Meade to come to them. Longstreet realized that Meade and his army held excellent defensive ground at Gettysburg and that the ensuing battle would be a bloodbath, which it was.

Lee would have none of it. He was wedded to his plan and entertained no contrary opinion from his most trusted subordinate. Instead, they attacked. On the last day of the battle, Lee ordered a frontal attack that became known as "Pickett's Charge." It ended disastrously for the Confederate Army and forced them to retreat.

The Confederate attack was also not well coordinated. While Lee gave his commanders broad discretion, he did not always make clear his intent, expecting his commanders to read his mind. As a result, during the battle, Lee's scouts failed to communicate intelligence on the Union troops' whereabouts, which left the Confederate Army unclear about Meade's positioning, which, in turn, delayed an attack on Meade's left flank. All of this led to the defeat at Gettysburg, where it's estimated Lee suffered a 54% casualty rate.

Many leadership lessons can be taken from this battle, and it is studied at the Army War College for this reason. However, that doesn't mean all officers learned from it. In World War II, Lieutenant General Mark Clark was the commanding general of the United States Fifth Army in Italy. The U.S. 36th Infantry Division under his command was ordered to cross the Gari River, with two regiments commanded by Major General Fred Walker.

Walker and others expressed doubts about the viability of the attack and strongly advised Clark to rethink the plan. Formidable German defenses awaited them across the river, making them sitting ducks. Attacking them head-on would be suicidal. In addition, the river was much higher than usual due to heavy rains, and constructing bridges would be more difficult. Despite this advice, a determined Clark ordered the attack to go ahead.

On the night of January 20, 1944, the U.S. fired an artillery barrage of 31,000 rounds on German positions across the Gari River, resulting in negligible damage because the German defenses were so strong and well-placed. After the barrage, two regiments from the U.S. 36th Infantry Division were ordered to cross the river. Despite valiant efforts, the crossing failed. Uncleared landmines, heavy return of German artillery fire, and high casualties of both men and landing boats were the leading causes.

The next day, Clark ordered both regiments to repeat the attack, even though little had changed. This time, the regiments managed to cross the river under the brutal German bombardment. But, maintaining their foothold on the other side proved unsustainable. Withering German fire prevented engineers from constructing pontoon and portable truss bridges. Without the bridges, armor couldn't cross, and the infantry was left to fight on its own. After more than 20 hours of fruitless combat and devastating casualties, both regiments were once again ordered to withdraw.

Most of one regiment had been left stranded on the wrong side of the river, and the Germans counterattacked, capturing hundreds of soldiers. The battle ended with no gains from either assault, only pointless American casualties and one of the largest defeats suffered by the U.S. Army during World War II. Clark had repeated the same mistakes Lee had made at the battle of Gettysburg.

Significant controversy followed this American defeat at the river Gari, and it was the subject of an investigation in 1946 by Congress to establish responsibility for the disaster. Although Clark's actions were upheld, many maintained the pointless battle was a result of his poor leadership. Clark prided himself on being a fearless and experienced commander, even though there was little evidence of this experience. What he had been good at was ingratiating himself with the Army hierarchy. Puffed up with his own importance, it isn't surprising that he had blustered ahead at the river Gari, learning nothing from others or the past. I have no doubt he studied past battles like the battle of Gettysburg in his training, but his ego prevented him from learning anything from it long before he reached the banks of the Gari river.

Learning can be achieved only if people are willing to admit they don't have all the answers and that others have something of value to share. There is no social learning if a person doesn't go through the process outlined earlier. This was certainly true of General Clark. His unwillingness to learn from others had an enormous cost in lives.

Knowledge is not finite; it's not the case that, once you've retained a certain amount, you've learned everything. There's always more to know. But when pride, ego, and insecurity get in the way of seeing learning as a positive and useful thing, forward momentum stops. This is a problem for leaders, since it is their job to move whatever work they're doing forward.

Why, then, is it hard for some leaders like Clark to learn from others? Because let's face it: the act of learning from other people takes place in a state of vulnerability. You put yourself in someone else's hands. You face possible judgment, ridicule, and uncertainty. Think how it feels on the first day of a new job, when you know nothing. How anxious that can be—to know that your fate rests in someone else's hands! No wonder the whole goal of learning becomes merely moving to less shaky ground for some people.

When I joined Target in 2012, I knew nothing about its supply chain or retail logistics. Nothing. I'd been hired ostensibly because of my leadership track record in the Army and because I'd done well enough in my interviews to convince senior leaders to hire me. I was placed in charge of a large distribution center, where I was expected to learn the business and lead the organization. Uncomfortable? Absolutely. But I was determined to succeed, and that depended wholly on me learning from others. I had to observe them, trust them, and, hopefully, grow with them.

Target had a great program to help with this process. My peers were supportive and coached me along the way. But I wasn't truly comfortable in my role with the company for a good 12 to 18 months after coming on board. Even then, more experienced peers could run circles around me. Only because I took note of less-than-successful peers and absorbed the behaviors, techniques, and business practices of the more successful ones did my confidence grow.

All leaders, good and bad, start out learning how to lead from others. Jack Welch, General Robert E. Lee, and General Mark Clark weren't born fully made leaders. They observed and emulated others along the way. But at some point, they stopped. They reached a point where, for whatever reason, they believed they'd arrived. No more shaky ground. They landed on a formula that worked and made them successful. Rinse and repeat.

So, let's go back to the beginning and the question about how we can tell which leaders are the right ones to study and emulate. I propose you should forget about character traits or measures of success. Instead, look for those leaders who are still learning—the ones who value and internalize the experiences of others, both alive and dead, and who aren't afraid to be vulnerable. If you look for that in a leader to model, all the other things will fall into place.

Then become a leader like that.

‹ ‹ ◆ › ›

−7−

BEING OPEN
TO OPPORTUNITIES

Vulnerability is
opportunity's wingman

There are many stories about doors not opened, paths not taken. Throughout the centuries, humans have been fascinated by the question of *What if? What if I had chosen differently?* Regret is all about the inability to give up the idea that life might have turned out another way. This can be a source of much anxiety. It puts a lot of pressure on the act of choosing. And this state of fear, anxiety, and uncertainty means that a person who must make a major life choice is going to be at a vulnerable crossroads.

The fact is, throughout your life, there will be these major decision points—opportunities that will either be taken or not. Most successful leaders can readily tell you about such singular moments that made a difference in their careers. Often these stories have a common thread. Despite unease, uncertainty, warring priorities, or other factors, these leaders opened themselves up to a possibility they didn't see before, an opportunity that changed the course of their lives.

Frequently when we talk about vulnerability, we focus on finding behaviors that will prevent a specific consequence, such as pain or harm, from happening. Rarely do we look at being vulnerable as a path to greater opportunity, but it can be. And I would argue that it is perhaps one of the key ingredients that will open unexpected doors for aspiring leaders.

In 1985, I felt my life was firming up nicely. I was a captain working at the Operations and Plans Directorate for the United States Army Military District of Washington, DC (MDW). I was recently remarried and full of ideas about my future—a future that didn't involve the U.S. Army. At that point, I'd met the requirement all ROTC scholarship recipients agree to—to serve at least four years on active duty—and I was halfway through a Master's degree in Administration, paid for largely by the Army. Given my job—steady hours, no deployments, and predictable weekends and nights to myself—it made sense to continue to serve until I had completed my master's. My new wife, Kim, had a promising career as a pediatric dietitian at Washington Children's Hospital in DC. We both thought finding work in the civilian sector would be more financially rewarding than staying in the Army. Only one of my many friends from college had gone into the Army; the rest were making money in various endeavors and had time to do things other than work. I felt envious and wanted the same latitude to work and play. We were in a "good spot" to move on to the next phase of our lives.

One day, as spring teased the earth and coaxed a rash of cherry blossoms to blush pink, I stepped out of the old brick building that housed my directorate. The air was cool and fresh, infused with the subtle fragrance of the blooms. The sun shone and flexed its emerging muscles. I stretched. My habit was to jog during my lunch hour along one of the running trails laid out in and around Fort McNair.

I was greeted by Glenn, a lieutenant colonel and Secretary of the General Staff for the MDW, who reported directly to the commanding general. The MDW headquarters didn't have a huge staff, so everyone was familiar with each other. I was a plans officer, and Glenn had been present during a recent briefing I gave to the MDW chief of staff regarding coordinating Army support for an upcoming exercise. Balding, remnants of reddish-gray hair neatly trimmed close, Glenn appeared more seasoned than his years. He had the keen focus of someone who didn't miss much, like an alert animal, taking in all the cues in the surrounding environment.

Sometimes in the Army, a briefing becomes an opportunity for senior staff to grill subordinates and try to trip them up. That was not the case with Glenn. He listened carefully and posed astute and relevant questions—the kind that suggested he saw all angles of a problem. He always treated others with unfailing respect. He struck me as a genuine person, one I wanted to know better. Over the course of many more briefings, we developed mutual respect for each other.

Out of the blue on this beautiful spring day, Glenn asked if he could join me for a run. Because the commute into DC required everyone to leave for work in the morning before the sun rose, most physical training happened during the day. Glenn belonged to the lunchtime crowd. Keeping physically fit is a part of Army life, especially for an officer. It's important to set a good example for the troops, and Glenn was no exception.

Dressed in civilian running attire—we were free to wear what we wanted when not part of a formation—Glenn stepped in beside me, and we soon fell into a syncopated rhythm. Everything about Glenn was spry and energetic. He had an easy stride. He matched mine, and yet subtly set the pace so that we pushed ourselves, as practiced runners do.

We took a trail through East Potomac Park, not far from Fort McNair, a fort built in 1791 and one of the oldest Army installations still in use. Established on the tip of a peninsula at the confluence of the Potomac and Anacostia Rivers, the fort includes picturesque trails along each bank, old brick buildings, and a view of the sleek Washington monument standing sentinel over the Capitol in the background. Saturated in history, the fort was the site of the imprisonment, trial, and hanging of John Wilkes Booth's four conspirators in Abraham Lincoln's assassination, including the first woman to be executed by the federal government.

As we ran, Glenn told me he'd been selected to assume command of a squadron in the 11th Armored Cavalry Regiment in Fulda, Germany, that upcoming summer. This wasn't a ho-hum assignment. The 11th was an elite, high-readiness unit poised geographically at the Fulda Gap, an area on the border between West and East Germany that contained two corridors of lowlands where tanks could be launched by the Soviet Union and its allies in a surprise attack. This was the shortest route to the middle of Germany and the Main River crossings, which, if secured by the Soviets, would sever West Germany from the NATO forces defending it. The 11th Calvary's mission was to remain on alert for such an attack and maintain constant surveillance of almost 400 kilometers of the Iron Curtain that separated East and West Germany. If the Soviets did attack, the 11ᵗʰ Cavalry would fight for time so that the units behind it could get into position.

Every officer in the Army was aware of the distinction between a command on the front line of the Cold War, on "Freedom's Frontier" (like the one Glenn had been selected for), and a job like mine behind the scenes at MDW. For lack of a better term, I was wallowing away, intending to resign my commission soon and pursue a career in the civilian world. The 11ᵗʰ had a history going back to 1901. It fought successfully for five years in Vietnam and produced numerous legendary commanders who later achieved general-officer rank in the Army. No question that Freedom's Frontier was the place for leaders who wanted a high-profile experience in a real-world unit, where, at any moment, war might break out. In 1985, about 300,000 troops were stationed in Germany, and it was where the action was.

Running down the blossom-strewn path, the Potomac glistening a bluish-green in the spring sun, Glenn turned to me and, without preamble, said, "Mike, I think you'd be a good fit for the 11ᵗʰ."

His offer took me by surprise. The 11ᵗʰ was a unit in the unique and respected cavalry component of the Armor branch, akin to the elite Ranger component of the Infantry. My assignments thus far had not been in cavalry, but in regular armor units as a platoon leader, company executive officer, and company commander—nothing that would single me out for this duty. Plus, I wasn't up for reassignment for another year. My intentions remained to resign my commission and pursue a career in the civilian world, ideally using my hard-earned chemical engineering degree from college.

Glenn proceeded to lay out, in a casual, almost offhand manner, the pros for me to make this move—the satisfaction of serving in an elite unit maintained at high readiness with the latest equipment, technology, and a day-to-day real-world mission, the opportunity to serve with some of the Army's best and rising leadership, and the unique chance to do something with my Army career. All this with the underlying message that he believed in me and had picked me from the scores of captains he could have chosen.

I glanced around at the others running and exercising in the park—military people and civilians escaping the confines of their office buildings for a moment, enjoying the beautiful day—and I felt that pulse-surging jolt of being given a remarkable opportunity. I knew a lot of things had to happen for me to accept the position, and I knew Glenn had plenty of other armor/cavalry captains to choose from.

Given all that, I should have jumped at it. But I didn't. What immediately came up for me were all the reasons I should say "No." The first major barrier that popped into my mind was my earlier conviction that I didn't want to make the Army my career. The second was whether my new wife would be willing to support a decision to go. It meant she would have to put her own career on pause. Third, stateside assignments like mine held a minimum requirement of two years, and I hadn't been in DC for even an entire year yet. Few exceptions were made to this rule, especially for captains, unless there were exigent circumstances, and there weren't any. Fourth, I had a year left to complete my master's degree. Fifth, Glenn was taking command in Germany that summer, and it was clear I wouldn't be able to join him until he was well into his command. And finally, and not least, I wondered if I could live up to his belief in me, whether I was the right material for this elite unit. I had an entire list of daunting reasons not to seize this opportunity.

What my mind did, like those of others faced with such a dilemma, was focus on obstacles and my potential shortcomings. It lobbied hard for me to take whatever steps necessary to prevent facing any pain, disappointment, regret, or embarrassment that such a decision might cause me in the future. In my mind, I had already mapped out my post-Army career path in the civilian world, one that I felt comfortable I could achieve without too many risks. The natural inclination, when people find themselves in a vulnerable position, is to do whatever they can, as quickly as they can, to get out of that situation.

To remain in a state of unease and anxiety is not comfortable, but it is the only way to override all of the reasons to say "No" to opportunity. To get to "Yes," it's necessary to be uncomfortable as long as it takes to make a clearer, more rational decision by weighing all the facts evenly. In other words, being in a state of uncertainty leaves people open to possibility.

For the next year, that's what I did—weighed the pros and cons, living in a state of uncertainty about my future. After much debate and soul-searching, my wife and I decided to go. We were a young, adventuresome couple with no kids given a chance to see Europe on the Army's dime, ready for new experiences, and intrigued about living in a foreign country. As an avid reader of military history, I found being stationed where some of the epic battles of the world wars had occurred particularly enticing. I promised Kim that, when I did leave the Army (we didn't know when, but possibly at the end of our tour in Germany), she'd be able to pursue her career as a dietitian.

It turned out to be a pivotal decision. I didn't get out after my 42 months in Germany. Instead, I found my calling and spent almost three more decades serving my country, finishing my 33-year Army career as a major general. That never would have happened had I immediately listened to all the reasons not to take the opportunity. This isn't to say I wouldn't have found success had I moved into the civilian sector, but I would have missed all the experiences that came as a result of this one choice.

I'm not advocating that you blindly take every opportunity that is presented to you, but rather that you allow yourself to marinate in a state of uncertainty instead of acting on your first instinct. *Let yourself be vulnerable.* Sometimes the right thing *is* to say "No." What's important is to make decisions not to escape some fear or unease or to rush to safe ground, but for legitimate reasons that have been examined in the face of your fears and doubts.

I'll use two examples to show the contrast. In January 1983, I attended the six-month Armor Officer Advanced Course at Fort Knox. All young lieutenants, upon commissioning, attend the Basic Course, where they learn about their branch and how the Army works, especially at the small-unit level—platoon and company. The Advanced Course comes next and teaches them about battalion and brigade operations, as well as logistics, and it also prepares them for company command. When captains leave the Advanced Course, they go into the field to pursue a command and also serve on a battalion and brigade staff.

In one of our first briefing sessions at the Advanced Course, one classmate stood out. His uniform leggings were stuffed into airborne boots, and he wore the maroon beret airborne soldiers sport. He had a certain confidence about him. He struck me as savvy, sure of himself, accomplished, and competent—the kind of guy I wanted to know. Afterward, we talked and hit it off. His name was Vance Richmond, and before long, we started hanging out. We shared many interests—both of us had recently been divorced, and we liked to work out, drink, and meet women (yes, we were young—in our 20s).

At that time, I'd made the decision to leave the Army after fulfilling my ROTC active-duty commitment and had already informed the Army. After spending a couple of months with Vance, I started to rethink these plans. He was so enthusiastic about the Army and his branch that he should have been a recruiter. His zeal was contagious. Sometime that spring, because of his influence, I contacted my branch and told them I'd changed my mind. I wanted to stay in the Army, go to Germany for my field command, and attend both the airborne and Ranger schools en route, just as Vance had. My branch was only too happy to comply, and soon it was all set up. I felt I had seized an opportunity that would take me places.

Then one weekend in March, Vance asked me to go on a road trip to visit his twin sisters, who lived in Kansas City. They were two years younger, and Vance was certain I would be a good match for one of them. He introduced me to Kim. She was petite, with dark-haired good looks, smart, and a lot of fun to be around. It wasn't long before I was taking that drive most weekends. From the start, I knew Kim was the right one for me. I had never been surer of anything in my life.

Suddenly, my decision to take the opportunity to go to Germany and the two schools seemed wrong. Obstacles reared up noisily in my mind. I feared that going to Germany for three years after airborne and Ranger school wasn't going to appeal to Kim and that she wouldn't wait for me. She had too much going for her. She'd recently completed her master's degree in nutrition. She was attractive, smart, and a great catch for any guy. I didn't believe that I would be enough to warrant the kind of commitment I'd have to ask from her. Still a bit insecure from my divorce, I was certain I would lose her. Even though we talked about it and she was supportive, I immediately rationalized her encouragement away, telling myself that she was new to the Army and didn't quite comprehend the ramifications.

Bottom line, being as smitten as I was, I didn't want to take any risks with our relationship. I backed out of the opportunity.

Vance convinced me to at least command as a captain before I got out instead of working some menial job at Fort Knox while waiting to resign my commission. So, I nixed airborne and Ranger schools, contacted the branch, and told them of my change of plans again. I asked to be sent to Korea for one year instead of three in Germany. My sole focus was to spend as little time apart from Kim as possible. Thankfully, I had a very accommodating assignment officer.

After Korea, Kim and I planned to get married and go some-where like Washington, DC, where I would resign my commission. We agreed it would be a good place for Kim to use her master's degree and work for one of the best children's hospitals in the country. We pretended this decision was a logical one, made with our future in mind, but in truth, it was a hasty, emotional decision on my part, based on fear of losing Kim. I wasn't willing to be vulnerable enough to admit this. My driving motivation was to minimize any risks. I didn't carefully weigh the pros and cons.

In hindsight, I lacked faith in myself and my future wife. My relationship with Kim had never been in jeopardy. She had more than shown her support. But I was unwilling to show how vulnerable I was when it came to marriage and my relationship with her. I preferred to try to control my external circumstances.

As a result, I turned down an opportunity that might have led me to find my calling much sooner than I did. It was a short-sighted, professional miss, one that I would have to overcome later in order to excel in my career. As mentioned earlier, Germany in the 1980s was the Army's driving focus, and I passed up a chance to be part of that. If I hadn't had the good fortune to meet Glenn in DC later, this mistake would have dead-ended my Army career.

Not going to airborne and Ranger schools meant I missed out on these two distinctions as a combat-arms officer. Both were "merit" badges that generated professional respect because they required going through a rigorous test of will, endurance, and commitment. Both schools meant completing challenging tests of physical and mental endurance, with substantial failure rates. Wearing those badges on your uniform meant something in a profession that valued these special skills. It surely would have been an opportunity for me to test my limits, risk failure, and learn about my own mettle. But since I passed on the opportunity, I will never know how I would have fared.

In contrast, years later, I chose not to accept another opportunity but with a very different mindset. At the time, I was the Assistant Chief of Staff for Operations, Plans, and Training (G3) for the 1st Cavalry Division in Bosnia-Herzegovina. This meant I had to coordinate the efforts of the entire division staff, from executing our deployment to developing plans for future operations in the country, briefing VIPs who visited, tracking all day-to-day operations, synchronizing the staff to move in the same direction, and doing whatever else needed attention operationally. I had my hand in everything, which was the nature of the job.

All operational deployments are tough because of their around-the-clock nature. Operations never sleep. Typically, I slept only four to five hours a night, and it wasn't unusual to be woken up in the middle of the night to handle some pressing issue. This deployment was particularly so because we were the first continental United States-based division to go to Bosnia-Herzegovina (the previous three had been based out of Germany). We were there to enforce and ensure compliance with the Dayton Peace Accords, crafted in 1995. A lot of attention was being paid to how we performed. The pace was relentless, never a dull moment. Plus, our division consisted of two U.S. brigades, an aviation brigade, a Turkish brigade, a Nordic-Polish brigade, and a Russian brigade, all working directly for us. My job would have been hard enough with only U.S. forces, but having all these international units included (there were other, smaller, units attached as well) made it even more challenging.

Every country had national caveats that restricted them from doing certain things or allowed them to do others. For example, the U.S. troops were not allowed to drink alcohol, but the Russian and Nordic-Polish brigades had no such restrictions and drank regularly. There were language issues. Other missions to apprehend people indicted for war crimes by the Hague were going on parallel to ours, and we had to coordinate with them. As in today's world, the Russians couldn't be trusted. It was challenging but also rewarding. As my first operational deployment, it was a true learning experience.

But I missed my family. The Army is tough on family life. It's not a nine-to-five job. Typically, even when stationed in the

States, roughly half of each year in command is spent away from home on training exercises or other pursuits. Most weekends also carry obligations—visiting the motor pool, checking barracks, preparing for the week ahead, reviewing training exercises, or acting as an observer-trainer for other units' exercises. Rarely was there a free, no-obligations Saturday and Sunday to hang out with family. Even before leaving for Bosnia, I spent three months away from my family preparing for the deployment. Because we had to wait for quarters, Kim and my two sons stayed with family in Omaha, while I moved to Fort Hood in Texas to train and prepare to deploy. I missed my son Nick's birthday and had just a week or two with them before I left for Bosnia in August 1998.

By the time I was deployed to Bosnia in 1998, my sons Nick and Tony were 10 and 8, and I'd been absent for about half of their birthdays, holidays, baseball and soccer games, and many other special events. And this was stateside. Being deployed overseas meant missing *all* of them.

While still in Bosnia in the spring of 1999, I received notification that I'd been selected for brigade/regimental command, a tough cut for any colonel to achieve. I was being considered for command of the 3rd Armored Cavalry Regiment, which was slated to deploy to Bosnia-Herzegovina the following summer. Since I was scheduled to come back from Bosnia that August, this meant that I would be home for less than a year before I would have to return.

My first reaction was to accept the command. This was a plum job that any armored cavalry colonel would be crazy to turn down. The regiment worked directly for a corps commander (lieutenant general), had a more varied, challenging mission profile, and was among the most highly resourced units in the

Army. It commanded great respect in my branch. Because of its elite status, many distinguished former commanders made general officer soon after they commanded the regiment. If I didn't take the opportunity, I'd be passing on a golden opportunity to be at the top of the heap among my peers.

At the same time, it would be another year of relentless work preparing to deploy and another year overseas, with little time for anything else, including my family. Having failed once in marriage, I was conscious of how important it was not to take those I loved for granted. I had to consider the hefty price to my family of accepting this exceptional assignment. I thought back about everything I had already missed with my boys, the burden I would put on my wife by asking her to be a temporary single parent yet again, and the many moments I would never get back with her.

I thought a lot about my own upbringing, how my father had been in many ways an absent father, like many men of his generation. He'd been so focused on his work, he'd come home every day exhausted and have a drink or two with my mother while the kids ate dinner separately. His only free times were the weekends, and his country-club memberships took him away golfing on most of them. My fondest memories of my dad are the rare times he did spend time with me. Like the time he coached me in Little League baseball when I was eight and nine and we lived in California. I didn't want my sons to be brought up the same way. I wanted to share as many moments with them as possible. Hopefully, they would remember these times fondly later in life. Unlike my father, I was not unaware of the cost of missing out on my children's lives.

So, I asked to be considered instead for another command stateside, specifically the 1st brigade combat team in the 1st Infantry

Division at Fort Riley, Kansas, which I knew was available. It had a great reputation and at the time was not in a deployment queue. It was an agonizing decision to make, especially given how much my 42 months in the 11th Armored Cavalry Regiment in Germany during the Cold War had meant to me in terms of professional development, pride in accomplishment, and membership. By asking not to be considered for command of the 3rd Regiment, I gave up professional prestige and the recognition that I was among the very best armor/cavalry colonels in the Army at the time. It was not an easy decision to make in a culture that glorifies such hallmarks. In the back of my mind, I was afraid I might be considered weak for turning such an opportunity down to be with my family.

Unlike my decision to bypass Germany and airborne and Ranger schools, I didn't make this choice out of fear. If I had, I would have chosen otherwise. Instead, I carefully weighed the pros and cons and consciously made the choice that benefited me and my family the most. I allowed myself to be vulnerable enough to admit what was true for me. I wanted to be as proud of being a father and husband as I was of being a colonel commanding in the United States Army. So, I passed on this opportunity with full knowledge. I gave up the prestige of a command with the 3rd Regiment and focused on being the best brigade commander I could be at my next assignment—and the best father as well.

And I can say that I have no regrets that I did.

When making major life decisions, one is inherently in a position of vulnerability. There is always risk involved in choice and, usually, where there is risk, there is fear. The key is to acknowledge this is the case and resist knee-jerk reactions that will unnecessarily close doors to opportunity and possibility. You must allow yourself to be vulnerable in the face of your fear. You must be vulnerable enough to figure out and admit what is true, and make your choice from that position. If you do, you will be less likely to regret your decision. I can promise there will be no second-guessing and no anguished *what-ifs*.

◂ ◂ ◆ ▸ ▸

–8–

BUILDING LOYALTY

*Vulnerability is the link between
trust and loyalty*

The idea of loyalty in business has changed over the years. People used to be loyal to a brand because they liked the product or were swayed by the advertising message. They knew little about what happened behind the scenes in the companies that made the products. Procuring the end product, not the process that led to obtaining it or the moral positions of the manufacturer, was what mattered. Likewise, employees were loyal to the companies they worked for because their employers provided a steady paycheck and were a part of the community. Employees were loyal to their bosses in the way they would be loyal to any authority whose decisions impacted their livelihood.

Now, with the rise of social media, new methods of marketing, and an enlightened workforce, all this has changed. Information that once was hidden is now available with the touch of a keyboard. The bar to getting and maintaining loyal customers and employees has risen. It's changed the way leaders must lead if they intend to be successful and develop a culture of loyalty.

I had a firsthand view of this at Target Corporation. Customers were not called "customers." They were "guests." The idea was that everyone who came into a store or purchased online should be treated like an honored guest in one's home. Instead of focusing on products, the company pivoted and homed in on the holistic customer experience. The major goal across all aspects of the organization was to sculpt guests' experiences to fit each individual's expectations. The thinking was that this type of experience would make customers loyal to the Target brand.

Every part of the company had its part to play. For example, in my supply chain area, our success was measured by how well we did our part in making the guest experience worthwhile and fulfilling. We routinely asked these questions of ourselves. Had we made sure each box contained precisely the right product and that each store had the right quantities, sizes, and colors? Were our deliveries on time? Was each trailer loaded correctly so that it took the least amount of time to unload, freeing up more time for store team members to devote to guests?

But this guest experience went far beyond the end-to-end process of each interaction. Part of the experience also included how Target was perceived as an entity on the planet. Our guests demanded transparency in how the company treated the environment, supported politicians, delivered on fair employment practices, and weighed in on many other social issues. To be competitive, Target—like other corporations—had to change, be more open. No longer could corporate activities be hidden behind flashy ad campaigns and pictures of multi-racial happy co-workers posed in idyllic work environments on the website.

This demand for transparency meant that corporations like Target were required to take some risks and become vulnerable, in order for their customers to trust them. Because, after all, trust is the bedrock of loyalty.

All of this means that the way we look at loyalty as leaders must change, too. With Target's overarching focus on the guest experience, employees were incentivized to meet metrics that truly put guests first. Loyalty to individual leaders was supplanted by loyalty to achieving guest-experience goals—meeting guest-serving metrics, improving processes so they become seamless, and ensuring high-functioning systems that consistently deliver.

Leaders, instead of calling the shots in isolation, needed to become guides and navigators, steering their teams to achieve these common guest-loyalty goals. They had to look for ways to lead teams that didn't include traditional authority, fear, whim, and ambition. They had to learn how to garner employee trust and loyalty differently. Loyalty was still an essential component of leadership—it is hard to lead if no one follows. It simply had to be approached in a different way.

Why is this important? Because loyalty is a basic human trait, necessary for all relationships, whether personal or professional. When true loyalty is established, it is usually based on trust, and one of the surest ways to inspire trust is to be vulnerable with one another.

Although loyalty is an abstract concept, there are several defining things about it:

1. There are many ways to be loyal, often a hierarchy of loyalties. Loyalty can be for another person, an institution,

a government, a cause, a higher purpose, beliefs, or one's values.

2. True loyalty is rarely a one-way street. To be loyal and inspire loyalty, both parties must be vulnerable, trusting, supportive, and devoted.

Let's break these ideas down.

What do I mean by a hierarchy? Human beings carry around with them many different types of loyalty: to truth, to their friends and family, to their God, to their organizations and institutions, and many other things. In any given circumstance, there can be competing loyalties. When this happens, not all carry equal weight. One loyalty is usually given greater importance over others and on down the line. As leaders, we must understand where we fit into this hierarchy of loyalty.

When I was the Executive Assistant to the Vice Chairman of the Joint Chiefs of Staff in the Pentagon, I had a window into these battling loyalties. The Joint Chiefs of Staff consists of the heads of each service—Army, Navy, Marines, Air Force, and National Guard—plus a Chairman and Vice Chairman. The Chairman reports to the Secretary of Defense. Whenever the Chairman travels, the Vice Chairman takes his place in Washington and represents and acts for him. For this reason, it wasn't unusual for my boss, the Vice Chairman, to meet frequently with the Secretary of Defense.

As his Executive Assistant, I managed the Vice Chairman's office—everything from scheduling to preparing briefings and information packets to coordinating with the rest of the staff. In other words, I was responsible for making sure my boss was informed and prepared for whatever came along and that his office was operating at the highest level of efficiency, effectiveness, and professionalism. It was a position of great responsibility and, frankly, prestige, but it also meant that if something went wrong, I would have to answer for it.

Once during the early part of the Iraq War, the Chairman left Washington, and my boss was called into a meeting convened by the Secretary of Defense. When the Vice Chairman came back from the meeting, his face was full of concern and troubled thought.

"Please come in." He nodded me toward his office. His tone was clipped, his lips grim, and I immediately wondered if I had screwed up. Normally, he was an engaging leader who never raised his voice or turned ugly. He had impressive composure, tact, and charm, but at that moment, I feared that was going to change.

My mind retraced everything I had done leading up to the meeting. Had I prepared him adequately? Had he shown up at the right time? Had I got the meeting location wrong?

I ushered myself into his office.

"Shut the door," he said.

At this point, I was firmly convinced I'd jacked something up. He rarely asked for closed-door meetings unless a sensitive or classified matter was involved or one of his supporting staff members was being discussed.

"Sit down." His tone was flat.

I sat stiffly in the chair in front of his desk and braced myself for an ass-chewing.

He looked me straight in the eyes. "I want to tell you something, Mike, and I don't want you ever to forget it."

"Yes, sir."

The meeting he'd attended with the Secretary of Defense had involved a certain policy initiative, and there had been an extensive and somewhat contentious discussion. My boss had delivered his input and questioned things he felt needed to be examined more closely about the policy. When the meeting broke up, the Secretary asked my boss to stay behind for a one-on-one follow-up. After everyone had left the room, the Secretary asked my boss if he could be counted on to support the direction in which the Secretary wanted to go. He asked if he could trust the Vice Chairman to "be on board."

My boss had been speechless for a moment. It was clear the Secretary was asking for an unconditional pledge of loyalty to him personally, for my boss to back the Secretary no matter what.

"I told him," my boss said to me, "that my job by law as the Vice Chairman is to provide you, Mr. Secretary, and the President with my best military advice, which I did."

He told the Secretary that he would support whatever direction was given to him by the Secretary, provided it wasn't illegal, immoral, or unethical. He knew that his job was not to make decisions; that was the Secretary of Defense's job. But the fact that the Secretary had questioned his loyalty and wanted to know if he could be trusted was disturbing.

He reminded the Secretary that he was loyal first to our Constitution, then to the offices of the President and the Secretary of Defense, but not to the Secretary personally. He reminded the Secretary that the Goldwater-Nichols Act of 1986 had codified this relationship between the Joint Chiefs and the Office of the Secretary of Defense, and that there was no misunderstanding on my boss's part about what his role and responsibilities were.

The Vice Chairman paused. "I'm telling you this, Mike, because you may be put in this situation in the future." He leaned forward. "Some of your superiors may want to extract an oath of loyalty to them. That is not what we pledged when we raised our right hands and accepted our commissions as officers in the military. Not what is reinforced each time we're promoted. Never forget our role when it comes to civilian control of the military—a foundation of how our government was designed. That is where our loyalty lies first and foremost. Never let anyone question your loyalty or demand trust where it is not warranted."

I left his office touched by his willingness to share this insight with me and clearer than ever about what loyalty meant, even after my own 24 years of service at that point. Although it's true that, in the military profession, one must be crystal clear about where loyalties and trust should and should not lie, it is not something that can be taken for granted. This is true in all aspects of our lives.

"Loyalty" can be a misplaced, misused word, and we must be clear about what deserves our loyalty and what does not. This does not mean that, as an officer, I couldn't be faithful to both the Constitution and a superior, but if the two should come into conflict, I would have to respect my hierarchy and choose the greater one. Hierarchy, then, drives how each of us shows our loyalty.

Everyone has heard the term "blind loyalty." This is when someone follows and supports a person or ideal in every circumstance without considering the loyalty hierarchy. It's done for both negative and positive reasons. Authoritarians and dictators often elicit loyalty through fear. People we respect and like can also make us blind because we want to be liked by them. Or we can turn myopic when we want to protect someone we care about. No matter the reason, the end result rarely benefits anyone.

At another point in my Army career, I was a major and assigned to a tank battalion to serve as the executive officer (XO), the second-in-charge. My new battalion commander and I had served together in Germany a few years beforehand. I liked and respected him. He had a real zeal for training and threw himself wholeheartedly into that aspect of leadership.

We'd been working together for only a few months because he was relinquishing command and moving on. During his remaining months, a comprehensive inspection was conducted by the division inspector general and his team. Often when a unit prepared for a new commander, inspections were conducted to see how well the various battalion systems—training, personnel management, logistics, intelligence, and maintenance—were working. It gave the new commander a baseline assessment for his new command.

Shortly before the inspection, the brigade commander (my boss's boss) asked me, as the second-in-command, to give him an opinion of how well the battalion systems were working and my overall impression. I told him everything was going well and that my boss had a good handle on all aspects of the operation.

The inspection revealed a different scenario. We didn't fare well. The battalion had issues that needed to be addressed, most of which I had been aware of when I gave the brigade commander my optimistic reassurances. He later pulled me aside and asked why my assessment didn't match the ensuing inspection report. I confessed that I hadn't been completely truthful because of a sense of loyalty to my boss, someone I'd served with before and with whom I had a close, personal relationship. I didn't want to say anything negative about him that might hurt his career.

Well, the brigade commander took that opportunity to counsel me about loyalty. He told me that, as Army professionals, we should be loyal to our units, the Constitution, Army values, and our soldiers but cautious about loyalty to individual leaders. It can be misplaced and even backfire. Instead of this blind loyalty to my boss, I should have been more forthcoming about the status of the unit. I should have answered the colonel's questions honestly, which I could have done without necessarily maligning my boss and his leadership. Glossing over issues was a risk to the readiness of the unit. That's what we as leaders were ultimately responsible for—ensuring that our soldiers and equipment were up to whatever task was given.

By sugarcoating the situation, I also did no favors for my battalion commander. A commander has to put his arms around all the systems in an Army unit. He can't pay attention to only the things he likes—in my boss's case, training—to the exclusion of all else. Commanders are responsible for the entire unit; the buck stops with them. If my white lie had let my boss slip by, he wouldn't have had the opportunity to shore up that weakness, and it would have hurt him in the long run.

The colonel pointed out that inspections were opportunities for leaders to learn where their weaknesses lie, so they can improve. No one is perfect. Good leaders acknowledge this and embrace their shortcomings as opportunities to fix problems. That's the key, he said. Problems should be considered a good thing—a learning opportunity.

It was a sobering conversation, reinforced many years later by the culture I became part of when I worked for Target, where having problems to work on was an expectation. It meant you had a handle on things and were aware of your organization's areas for improvement. Mature leaders who are confident and have good people working for them willingly acknowledge their challenges and have plans to address them. My brigade commander made that clear to me, and I understood that blind loyalty to a friend served no one—not the individual, not the unit, not the Army, not me. In the hierarchy of loyalty, almost always, loyalty to individuals is trumped by loyalty to the greater good.

Which brings me to my second point about loyalty. It is never a one-way street. If leaders take nothing away from the subject other than this, it will serve them well. Simply having a title and a position of authority does not guarantee loyalty. Especially in our changing world.

First, leaders must be clear about their team's shared loyalties. In the Army, at the top of the hierarchy lies being true to the Constitution and the unit. In Target, our shared loyalty priority was the guest experience. Good leaders in any organization will exhibit and unfailingly support these shared loyalties. They will set the example.

Second, a leader must be able to garner trust, the basis upon which all loyalty is built. Before people trust a leader, they must know the leader will not betray, abuse, disrespect, or dismiss them—and that the leader has their best interests at heart. To do this, leaders must be both vulnerable and transparent. Show that they are human. That they don't have all the answers. Show they need others' help and care. Many leaders are afraid that, by doing this, they will be perceived as weak and lose their authority. But authority alone is never enough. Trust must be established, which happens when human beings are vulnerable with each other. Only after that will loyalty follow.

Third, leaders must support and celebrate members of their team in the same way they expect their teams to support them. This means a leader must be able to step aside and let others shine. Leaders must show they understand and care about the problems and issues team members face.

Think about bosses to whom you felt deeply loyal. My guess is that they checked all of these boxes. Think about the things they did that made them different from other leaders who didn't inspire such loyalty. Then emulate them.

In my case, one such boss was Major General William Hartzog, Division Commander of the 1st Infantry Division at Fort Riley. At the time, I was a major and one of the division plans officers, responsible for writing and vetting tactical operations plans. During division-level training exercises, a series of trucks with workspaces mounted on the back would be set up as the command post in the field. They would be configured so that all the staff—operations, plans, intelligence, logistics, and signal—could easily interact.

We'd be slaving away late at night in our truck-mounted van, writing plans for an upcoming operation, and Major General Hartzog would wander in. He'd sit down and talk—sometimes for an hour. He'd talk to us about our careers, offer us assignment advice, ask about our families, and make a genuine effort to get to know us. He'd stand in front of a whiteboard and teach us about division tactics, what he'd seen work for him in the past, and what had been failures. Marker in hand, he'd school us based on his experiences and share how he liked to operate.

Before this, in my experience, interactions with senior officers had been a bit perfunctory, managed, and brief. Not that these leaders didn't care. It was more that their priorities were elsewhere. So, a major general coming into a van late at night simply to talk to younger officers, with no agenda and no one feeding him questions, was a novel experience. It made me feel noticed. That what I did mattered. That we were all in it together. He sincerely wanted to know what was happening and what our concerns were.

Later, when I became a general, I remembered those late nights with Major General Hartzog. I made a point to put into practice what I'd learned from him. During my commands at both Fort Knox and Fort Jackson, I had my hair cut every Saturday morning. I asked the barber on post to open a little early, and I talked with her alone while she cut my hair. Since she cut soldiers' hair every day of the week, she knew everything that happened on post. She heard a lot. I didn't interrogate her, but I casually worked the conversation around to the scuttlebutt. When she opened for business, I went on my way, no one the wiser.

I took that information—things like the quality of the food in the dining facility, what was being said about commanders or units, problems with the staff at the fitness center, or whatever was on the troops' minds—and used it to quietly get to the bottom of the issues and, if warranted, do something about them—all with no fingerprints. Those nights with Hartzog made me realize that if you want to get to the truth of something, want to understand what really is going on, you have to go all the way down the chain of command. Because by the time information usually comes all the way up, it's been filtered and scrubbed and sanitized.

When I was a lieutenant colonel a bit later in my career, another general officer inspired me to put something else into practice. I would block time on my calendar and free myself to go where my instincts told me to go, based on the unit's various activities. As a brigade commander, and then as a general, I'd take this time to check on the state of affairs, mostly training, but also maintenance activities, supply centers, and other places on post. The purpose of my unannounced visits wasn't to play "gotcha," but to see things as they really were, without the dog-and-pony preparation that so often precedes high-level visits. It was an opportunity for me to get feedback from the troops without any filters, create a two-way street. I didn't advertise where I was going, and it drove my subordinate commanders crazy. They'd pump my aide de camp for details about my destination, in case it was an area under their responsibility. But he'd never divulged where I was going.

After a while, they began to understand that these visits were to benefit them and their units. I wasn't there to punish anyone; I was there to support them. They relaxed, and we had discussions about what I observed and heard. I shared with them my own experiences, mistakes I'd made, and anecdotes, doing my best to remove the curtain of hierarchy. In the end, they used information from these discussions to take whatever actions they felt were appropriate to improve their units. If it wasn't yet part of how they led, they soon took up this practice themselves, going out to see firsthand what was going on in their units.

When I retired, I was told by those I'd worked for that I was a soldier's general, someone who took a genuine interest in the people at the lowest end of the totem pole, someone who wanted to know what I could do for them. I strongly believe that this is the surest way for leaders to build loyalty and trust.

Without a two-way street, without understanding the shared hierarchy of values between people working or living together, and without being vulnerable enough to establish trust, it is impossible to build loyalty. In today's world, where a title and assigned authority are not enough to inspire loyalty, a leader must be the keeper of these shared values and must nurture and shepherd them. Most important, leaders should never demand trust or loyalty for their own personal goals or benefit.

‹ ◂ ◆ ▸ ›

−9−

UNDERSTANDING
EMOTION

*Vulnerability means harnessing
emotion*

Scientists haven't yet been able to create artificial intelligence that mirrors human thought exactly, because many of our decisions are not based solely on hard facts and logical reasoning. A large part of human thought is created, influenced, or activated by emotion. Interactions between human beings usually include some type of emotion.

Since the 1970s, it has been generally believed that there are six basic human emotions: happiness, sadness, fear, disgust, anger, and surprise. However, in 2017, a UC Berkeley study challenged this view. It compiled responses to more than 2,000 emotionally evocative video clips from more than 800 men and women. The researchers found that emotions were not isolated but often connected with each other. Instead of half a dozen, there were 27 distinct categories of emotion. These included admiration, adoration, aesthetic appreciation, amusement, anger, anxiety, awe, awkwardness, boredom, calmness, confusion, contempt, craving, disappointment, disgust, empathic pain, entrancement, envy, excitement, fear, guilt, horror, interest, joy, nostalgia, pride, relief, romance, sadness, satisfaction, sexual desire, surprise, sympathy, and triumph. The study specifically classified them as categories because we have many other words which describe specific emotional states that are related to one of these 27, such as the term "bittersweet," which is often used when referring to nostalgia.

In her book *Atlas of the Heart,* Brené Brown claims there are even more—87 different emotions plus infinite possibilities because, at any given time, a person can experience a mix of emotions. But, whatever the ultimate number of human emotions is, most experts agree the mind tends to assign a negative or positive value to each one. Happiness is good. Fear is bad. Not surprisingly, showing negative emotions is often equated with exhibiting weakness or showing character flaws. We've grown up in a culture that doesn't encourage emotional expression, especially when it's deemed negative. As a result, showing these "negative" emotions often puts us in a vulnerable state.

As we've discussed in previous chapters, the most common emotions that accompany vulnerability are fear and uncertainty, but there are others. For example, when someone is sad or feeling guilty, they can feel vulnerable. And when someone feels that way, they're often reluctant to admit experiencing whatever emotion they have because it leaves them exposed.

The workplace is a particularly unfriendly place for expressing this type of emotion. A friend of mine who was a Vice President in the financial services industry told me that she received a phone call at work one day. A friend of hers had committed suicide.

Stunned, she hung up and stood for a few minutes looking out the window, tears in her eyes. Her boss chose that moment to drop in. When she turned, signs of crying were clearly noticeable, and he nearly recoiled. He held up his hand and said, "You're not going soft on me, too, are you?" referring to another woman who had recently been upset in a staff meeting. Before my friend could respond, he retreated, telling her, "I'll come back when you've pulled yourself together."

In our society, women tend to express their emotions more easily; men have been indoctrinated that to do so is unmanly and cowardly. Zippia, a career-resource company, reports that 64.4% of business leaders in the U.S. are men. So, it is not surprising that my friend had a male boss who behaved this way. The message he gave her was that leaders don't show emotion at work for any reason. Leaders must appear invulnerable at all times. My friend told me that the entire time she worked for the company, she felt alienated; she eventually left the industry altogether.

Leaders who aren't afraid to show their vulnerability openly acknowledge the emotions they feel and give the people who work for them the freedom to do likewise. Emotional expression is part of vulnerability. If this freedom isn't a part of the workplace culture, talented potential leaders will feel the same way my friend did and go elsewhere. This is one of the reasons it is especially important for leaders to understand how emotions should be exhibited and handled during working hours.

Obviously, of the 27 different categories of emotions, some should not be brought into the workplace—contempt and sexual desire, for example. But for the most part, both employees and leaders should be able to express their emotions and the accompanying moments of vulnerability, as long as they do so in a constructive manner. Leaders must know how to model and teach the right way to express these emotions.

To illustrate what I mean by "constructive," let's talk about guilt and shame, terms often used interchangeably. In *Atlas of the Heart,* Brené Brown points out that the two are not the same at all. "What's interesting is guilt gets a really bad rap, but guilt is a very socially adaptive emotion. Guilt is 'I did something bad,' and shame is 'I am that.'"

She goes on to explain that shame labels a person as bad, unworthy, and unlovable. People feeling this emotion suffer, and there is nothing to be done because it is not about whatever happened, but about the people themselves. Shame often leaves no opening for resolving what happened; it only creates blame and contempt. On the other hand, people feeling guilt admit they did something wrong and take steps to make amends. It doesn't make them bad people who are unworthy of love. Guilty people take responsibility for the mistakes they make and clean up the fallout.

As a leader, it is highly likely that you'll do something or make a decision you regret—some that end badly and maybe hurt other people. You'll be in the very vulnerable position of having to acknowledge you are the person responsible for the mistake. Likely, you will feel guilt or shame in that situation, one of which will be constructive, the other not.

When I was in Iraq, one of my duties was to administer a camp outside of Baghdad called Camp Taji. About 15,000 troops were in the camp, and I was responsible for coordinating security, housing, life support, and other basic operations. It was a temporary base for some of the units coming into and out of Iraq, and I spent a night or two each week at the camp.

On one of my trips from Baghdad to Camp Taji, the helicopters were grounded due to a severe sandstorm. We had to drive instead. It was about a three-hour trip through an area of Baghdad province where there'd been a lot of recent IED (improvised explosive device) activity. Whenever generals traveled in Iraq, they typically went with a security detail in four up-armored vehicles—Mine Resistant Armor Protected combat vehicles (MRAP), the most protected transportation available. My four-vehicle team assessed the enemy situation, came up with a route, gathered intel, and planned contingencies before we set off. I rode in the second vehicle of the procession with my driver, Specialist (SPC) Baskis, and another NCO.

Although it was a tense ride up to Camp Taji, we made it without incident. Shortly after arriving, my NCO in charge got word from Baghdad that mandatory training had to be conducted as soon as possible (some division headquarters' requirement). They wanted my security team to turn around and head back to Baghdad that same afternoon for the training. I was not pleased with the development, given that my team faced potential danger and storm conditions. But I reasoned that I really didn't need them for the few days I'd be at Camp Taji, and we'd managed the trip there without incident.

Against my better judgment, I reluctantly approved their departure.

They grabbed some chow and headed back. My NCO in charge moved up to the lead vehicle. SPC Baskis drove the second vehicle as usual, and another NCO, Sergeant Victor Cota, sat in the passenger seat. Usually at mealtimes, I tried to share a meal with a young soldier or two, check on their well-being, and ask how their families were doing. That morning, I'd had breakfast with Sergeant Cota. He was in his late twenties. A stocky but solid soldier of Hispanic origin, he had an air of quiet competence about him. I asked him about his sons. He had two, aged four and seven. As we talked, he took a hard-boiled egg and set it on his tray. He gently rolled it under his palm. Back and forth, back and forth until the shell cracked and he could peel it. I'd never seen anyone crack an egg like that. Very efficient, like an expert. Even to this day, that's how I do it.

About 10 minutes out from Camp Taji, my security team was struck by a massive IED. The device and the wire that led to a detonator about 200 yards away had been camouflaged; it was a well-executed attack. The fact that our vehicles were MRAPs meant little. A projectile formed by the explosive hit the passenger side door of the second vehicle and blew right through it. Sergeant Cota was killed instantly, blown in half. The projectile went through him and then struck the frame of the vehicle right above SPC Baskis's head. The impact fragmented the projectile and lacerated his face and neck profoundly. The blast concussion itself was so powerful that it fractured the orbital bones around both of his eyes and blinded him.

Fortunately, no one else in the convoy was injured.

The remainder of my security team did what they could on the ground. They called Division operations in Baghdad for an air medevac, the only helicopters allowed to fly in the storm. News of the attack reached the division commander and chief of staff, who assumed I was with the vehicles. They frantically tried to confirm what had happened, thinking I'd been hit. When they realized I wasn't with the formation, they tracked me down at Camp Taji.

It was the worst call I've ever received. Everything stood still. I thought about Sergeant Cota that morning at breakfast—his earnest, intelligent smile. A single thought ran through my mind. *I should never have let them go.*

I knew I had to get to the explosion site. I managed to gather up enough vehicles to make the trip, and we left immediately, arriving 30 minutes later. Just in time to see the medevac bird take off. I missed seeing SPC Baskis and Sergeant Cota. The rest of my team hung around at the site, dejected and shocked. I looked around at each face, sorrier than I'd ever been. My decision had done this to them.

The next day, I attended the ramp ceremony at Baghdad International Airport, where Sergeant Cota's remains were loaded via casket onto a U.S. Air Force transport plane for its trip back to Dover, Delaware. There is nothing more somber and gut-wrenching than a flag-draped coffin heading home. No apology or remorse could ease the sorrow waiting for it at the other end. Again, I thought, *I should never have let them go.*

I flew to Balad Air Force Base, which was where a major U.S. military hospital was located. I visited SPC Baskis. He had definitely lost one eye, and the doctors weren't sure about the other, but they said he'd likely lose it as well. He did and was blind for life. I awarded him a Purple Heart and a Combat Infantryman's Badge (what an infantry soldier gets when in combat). It was poor compensation for all that he had lost.

Through all this time, the thought uppermost in my mind was that my decision had resulted in this. It hadn't been critical for my security team to return to Baghdad for training. If I'd gone with my gut, relied on my instincts, they wouldn't have been hit. Sergeant Cota wouldn't be dead. Specialist Baskis wouldn't be blind.

What I felt was guilt—raw remorse. I'd made the wrong decision, and people's lives had been irreversibly impacted. Until this day, the people who suffered because of my decision are never far from my mind. But I didn't believe my mistake meant I was a bad person, that something in me was rotten. My decision-making on that day had been flawed. But that didn't mean that I would *always* make bad choices or that I couldn't contribute good to the world moving forward. I focused not on the regret I felt but on what I could do to make amends to SPC Baskis's and Sergeant Cota's families for my mistake. It was not about me.

The day after the attack, we held a memorial service for Sergeant Cota at our headquarters. I eulogized him. Even though he didn't work directly for me, he was under my command, and I felt it was the least I could do. I wanted to be personally responsible for making others understand exactly who this promising young man was. I reached out to his wife to make sure her family received the support they needed from the Army's Casualty Affairs personnel—help with grieving, prompt payment of her husband's life insurance, and other types of assistance. I maintained contact with her for a few years after the incident, checking in periodically.

I did the same for SPC Baskis. Over the years, he has dealt with his blindness in a remarkably positive way—by becoming an established author, presenter, athlete, and motivator. In 2013, he was awarded the Louis Braille Award for his inspirational impact on other blind people. He medaled at the national level in the summer and winter Paralympics and has his own podcast (Baskis 360). He established a nonprofit called Blind Endeavors, which I support. He is an amazing example of resilience. I consider myself lucky to have known this inspirational young man.

What this illustrates is that guilt allows the focus to be on the future for all parties. No one can change an action taken or a decision made, no matter how desperately one wishes. Guilt focuses the attention on the person hurt or wronged.

On the other hand, shame leaves people stuck in the past.

At another time, in July 2004, I was getting ready to deploy to Kuwait as a newly minted brigadier general in support of our wars in Iraq and Afghanistan. The situation was very fluid at the time, particularly in Iraq, where the terrorists were becoming more lethal, security was deteriorating rapidly, and units were having their stays extended. I knew I was in for a challenging year, and it was on my mind as I readied myself for the next 12 months.

At the same time, my older son, Nick, was not exactly thriving as a soon-to-be junior in high school. Smart, engaging, and popular, he largely rejected studying in favor of partying, and like many adolescents, was increasingly aloof, especially from me. At the time, I didn't realize that his behavior was typical of most teenage boys. I thought only of the impact it had on me and how it made me feel as I prepared for a stressful overseas assignment in a combat theater of war. I didn't relish the idea of leaving my wife, who would be a single parent yet again, with the burden of handling a rebellious teenager for another year. As a result, resentment built, and I deployed carrying it with me.

While I was in Kuwait, I missed Nick's entire junior year of high school and all the acting out that went with it. My wife, Kim, was working full-time at Washington Children's Hospital as a pediatric dietitian, which involved an hour or more commute at each end of the day. Not only did she have to juggle taking care of a sulky junior with her demanding job, but she also had to supervise our other son as well.

Nick took full advantage of the situation. He brought home substandard grades. He ratcheted up his misbehavior and got caught by the police numerous times for drinking, smoking dope, and other teenage antics. Thankfully, the police officers were somewhat understanding, and he avoided being arrested. Instead, they periodically woke my wife up with late-night notifications that he'd yet again done something that put him on their radar. You can imagine how stressful the situation was for her.

When we discussed these incidents involving Nick long distance, I found myself getting angrier and angrier. I was miles away, unable to help, and the idea that he would do this to his mother enraged me. She cautioned me emphatically that getting upset with him and unloading on him when I got home was the last thing I should do. It would only further alienate us from our son and exacerbate the situation. I agreed with her.

Before returning home, I thought through various strategies I could employ to renew my relationship with Nick and have some influence on him. I wanted him to understand that he was going down a road he would later regret, that he was seriously compromising his chances of getting into a good college, and that I knew he was a better student and a better son than he was showing. By the time I headed home, I felt I had control of my emotions and knew how to handle the situation.

About two days after I returned, I went with my wife and our boys to a hardware store to pick up some things I needed for a home-improvement project. We got out of the car in the parking lot. Nick was acting sullen and aloof. He clearly wanted to be anywhere except with his family. For two days, he'd shown few signs of having missed me while I was gone, and it rankled. Still feeling the effects of jet lag and wanting us to be the united, happy family we obviously weren't, I lost it with him on the spot.

My voice is loud and tends to carry, so everyone in the parking lot could hear what I said to my son. I yelled at him for putting his mother through the stress he'd caused while I was gone. I said some nasty things—such as he was a worthless piece of crap. I told him I should knock some sense into him (I'd never laid a hand on either of my sons), that he was a real moron for getting caught by the police—not once or twice but three times, and that he and his worthless friends were losers. My wife had to intervene. It was one of those scenes that makes everyone in the vicinity cringe and turn away.

My son said nothing. I can remember the way he looked at me, both alarm and resentment in his eyes.

We didn't go into the store. We piled back into the car and rode home in total silence. At the steering wheel, I was still fuming. I was so angry that my blood pressure was likely off the charts, and my hands were visibly shaking.

When I eventually calmed down, my wife confronted me about my behavior. She was crying. She'd carefully planned a homecoming, as she did each time I came back from a deployment. Most people don't realize how difficult reintegrating back into family life is after an extended absence. The spouse at home deals with everything for a year on their own—kid issues, work, running the household, school events, and home repairs. They develop a routine, and then the spouse blasts through the front door and disrupts it. Often the soldier comes home carrying baggage from any nastiness he saw while deployed. So, Kim had planned some great meals, organized activities for the family to do together, and tried to set things up so that we could gradually ease back into a family routine.

And I had come back home with the expectation of resuming charge of things and telling everyone how it should be. In the hardware-store parking lot, I'd blown to smithereens all her plans for a smooth transition.

And worst of all, I had treated my son with loathing and contempt. He was simply going through a process that most teenage boys go through at that age. My brother-in-law, a noted child psychologist, later explained the stages of growing up to me and gently suggested that my reaction to Nick had been, frankly, poor parenting.

As my wife talked to me that day and laid out the impact of my behavior on her and my sons, I felt shame. I hated myself. I thought I was a bad husband and father. My behavior reminded me of my own dad and the things he'd said to me when I was Nick's age—shouting, face beet red, threatening to hit me, calling me a worthless piece of crap—exactly as I had behaved with Nick. As my father's target, I remember feeling resentful, belittled, and misunderstood. I didn't want to be around him. I avoided him.

Now, my son was looking at me that way.

At that moment, I truly despised myself. I was ashamed of having totally screwed up what should have been a joyous, unifying event—my return home from a year-long deployment. Something was wrong with me. I thought I didn't deserve to be part of the family. I was convinced they didn't want to be near such a shitty father and husband. If I weren't there, their lives would be better. I told my wife that the best solution would be for me to move out.

Luckily, Kim talked me through it. I realized that leaving would not repair the situation with my son. In fact, it would worsen it. It would validate that I was the awful person I thought I was and would turn the situation into a self-fulfilling prophecy. What I would leave my son with was that vision of me at my worst in the parking lot.

With the help of my wife, I was able to shift my shame into guilt and do the things I needed to move forward and have the type of relationship I wanted with my sons and my wife. Although I'm not proud of my behavior that day, I wasn't the first father to melt down and say things he regretted. What mattered was taking responsibility for it and acting differently moving forward.

After that day, I started trying to see the world through my sons' eyes, to listen to them more, to admit my foibles and weaknesses, and to focus more on them than myself. I continued my dialogue with my brother-in-law to better understand what life was like for teenage boys, especially Army brats, with all the associated disruptions. Today, I would not trade my relationship with my sons for anything.

The whole point is that it's important for everyone to understand how emotions drive us when we are at our most vulnerable. Turning those emotions into constructive expression provides space for everyone to focus on moving forward, repairing what has been broken or lost, and reinforcing relationships that form the core of any group.

A leader's job is to help steer people to this understanding—to be much like my wife, Kim, was when I was in the grip of shame. She helped move me from a place where I wallowed in my emotion to a place where I could see what actions I needed to take. She gave me the room to express my emotions in a way that was constructive for our whole family, just as good leaders always keep an eye out for the health of the whole team. The more leaders understand the power of emotion and its consequences, the more likely they will model the right type of behavior and help team members to do so as well.

‹ ◂ ◆ ▸ ›

− 10 −

MASTERING FEEDBACK

Good feedback is an act of
vulnerability on both sides

Human nature being what it is, it is difficult for us to honestly assess our own behavior. We see our actions through internal filters that may or may not be accurate. We tell a joke and think we are hilarious. We give a talk and assume we're brilliant. We make a mistake and believe we're the most incompetent person in the world. Not until we receive external feedback are we able to see a more balanced view of our behavior. When nobody laughs at our jokes, we recalibrate our view of being funny. People fall asleep during our talk, and we rethink our brilliance. Our boss tells us he made the same mistake starting out, and we understand that we are as competent as the next person.

If only it were that simple!

Giving and receiving good feedback is not a genetically transmitted trait. It's a skill we must learn and master. And it's fraught with multiple ways of going wrong. Why? Because we often feel vulnerable when we're on either end of this kind of discussion.

A person receiving feedback might immediately become defensive and believe they are being criticized or picked on. They might interpret what is said to mean they're not worthy or appreciated. On the other hand, the person giving feedback might be afraid of jeopardizing a relationship by saying something honest, for fear the other person won't like it. Or they can worry that there'll be negative repercussions from someone who is in a more powerful position.

In any case, feedback often leaves people feeling exposed.

In the traditional work setting of the past, feedback was one-way and occurred once a year during a performance appraisal—if at all. Over the years, organizations have tried to change this by implementing processes such as 360° performance appraisals, where reviews are provided not just from a boss to an employee, but also from subordinates to bosses, from one peer to another, and from co-workers in different departments to each other. This kind of performance review tries to capture the full performance picture. While this is laudable, it doesn't address the issue that many people who review each other don't know how to give effective feedback, and many don't know how to receive it. A performance review is effective only if its contents work and there is follow-up.

The Army put a 360° program in place a few years before I retired in 2012, but it was anonymous. It also lacked the context that person-to-person discussion provides. Personally, I found it to be of minimal value and not a driver of behavior change. Why? Because the feedback was academic in nature, its impact on the recipient was unknown, and the results it produced were indeterminate. Unless feedback is ingrained in an organization's culture, where giving and receiving it is an expectation and closely tied to developmental programs, it will likely fail to achieve the desired results.

So, simply implementing a 360° process is not enough. What also needs to be present are leaders who model and instruct their teams on *how* to give good feedback, no matter what program is in place in the organization.

There are often a number of things working against companies tasked with creating an environment conducive to valuable feedback. The first is the organization's culture. If an organization is top-down, hierarchical, and authoritative, it is extremely difficult to create a space for effective feedback. The culture is set up to support only results-focused, one-way communication. Second, the *myth of the title* often creates barriers. By this, I mean real or inherent titles that put leaders on pedestals—such as "President," "CEO," "Vice President," "General," "movie star," or "talk-show host"—can tamp down the willingness of subordinates to give honest feedback. Third, feedback doesn't flourish easily in organizations run by an authoritarian who leads by whim and edict. Picture the king in the story *The Emperor's New Clothes* whose courtiers fear upsetting him so much they won't even tell him he's naked. Finally, a litigious environment, where formal complaints and lawsuits are a go-to response to any slight or misunderstanding, doesn't bode well for implementing a robust evaluation culture. While these situations make it more difficult, good leaders can work within their own sphere of influence to model how to provide worthwhile feedback outside of the formal process.

Leaders should keep in mind that the goal of feedback is to deliver a specific message to an employee, boss, peer, or co-worker when they have been observed doing something well or something that needs improvement. It should be delivered in a way that leaves no doubt about what activity or situation the communication refers to, what specific behaviors were observed, and the impact those behaviors had on either the organization or the individual who provided the feedback.

Again, it sounds simple, but it's surprising how often these messages can miss their mark.

When feedback isn't specific, it leaves a person unsure and unable to definitively replicate/modify whatever success/failure has occurred. Vague feedback only makes people second-guess themselves or leaves them looking for hints to understand what the communication meant. The person is left to put their own spin on the message they received and make their own assessment of their behavior, which may or may not be useful.

As I've mentioned before, the Army is a very hierarchical organization, and appraisals tend to be one-way. Some of the most brilliant leaders I encountered were short on providing feedback, especially the positive kind.

I remember once when I'd been selected for promotion to major but hadn't yet pinned on the new rank. I was a senior captain and operations officer in a squadron in the 11th Armor Cavalry Regiment in Germany. I was reassigned out of my squadron and made an adjutant or military administrative assistant for the regimental commander at his headquarters. At the time, I wasn't told why the move was being made. I believed I was being taken out of a plum job to fill an uninteresting role at headquarters. My desire was to be in the midst of anything having to do with operations, plans, and training—my comfort zone. A regimental adjutant, on the other hand, was more focused on administration, personnel, moving paperwork, and protocol—important functions, but not my cup of tea.

For this reason, I went into my new job with a cloud over my head. I didn't throw myself into my work wholeheartedly. The regimental commander I worked for was a highly decorated Vietnam War veteran who had moved up quickly in the Army because of his sterling reputation. He got results. He was both arrogant and enigmatic, oftentimes charismatic, and I had a hard time reading him.

Known to be tough and demanding when it came to subordinates, and rarely providing positive feedback, he presented a challenge. He often waited until the last minute to make decisions, which kept everyone guessing. I later found out he did this on purpose. He reasoned that combat was similar. By waiting until the last moment, he felt he was training his subordinates to think on their feet, be adaptable, deal with contingencies, and act quickly on little information. But at the time, I didn't know this.

As his adjutant, I was a jack of all trades and did whatever he asked of me, on call at his every whim, or at least that's what it seemed like to me. Part of my job was to help him with all the paperwork that came into his office—correspondence, promotion orders, scheduling requests, disciplinary actions, you name it. He was notorious for ignoring the mounds of growing documents and missives. Then, out of nowhere, with a burst of energy and frequent complaints, he'd plow through it in one sitting. One day he called me into his office and said, "Look at this." He pointed to his inbox, which was overflowing. "You're not doing your job. Come up with a better system."

In response, I created three inboxes—one "hot," one "medium," and one "cold," so he'd know what items needed to be addressed immediately and what could wait. I would manage the boxes for him to ensure nothing went stale or missed a deadline. But it didn't solve the problem. The "hot" box began to fill up and remain unattended. Clearly, my solution wasn't what he wanted. I was at my wit's end. I had no idea what he expected of me. He gave me no feedback. The only thing I knew for certain was that he wasn't happy and that I wasn't quite cutting it. I grew more frustrated.

Even though I was his adjutant, I didn't report directly to him. Returning to my office one day, I overheard my direct boss, the regimental executive officer, talking to the regimental commander, who groused, "He isn't doing this right or that." At first, I thought he was talking about somebody else and felt bad for the officer—until I heard the inbox as part of the litany of things done wrong and then my name tossed out. My reaction was *Holy crap, he's talking about me.* The vein in my temple started pounding.

My boss left the commander's office and walked into mine. Things didn't look good for me. He let me know the commander was unhappy with my performance and that there were concerns about my ability to do the job. "Mike," he said. "You need to take some leave. Say, for about a week. We'll talk about it when you get back."

So, my wife, our 15-month-old son, Nick, and I took a vacation for a week. The whole time I was certain I'd be fired when I returned. The idea stung. Thus far, I'd been successful in all the jobs I'd taken on. Even though I'd been lukewarm about the job in the first place, I felt that the issues were not solely my fault. Nevertheless, I had come up short in an important role, and being relieved or reassigned to a lesser job would not exactly be a career-enhancing move. You can imagine the pins and needles I was on when I returned.

But my boss had used the week to smooth things over with the commander. He'd known him for several years and helped me tighten up my act by explaining specifically what I needed to do to satisfy the commander. He gave me specific feedback on how to respond to the commander's requests such as handling the inbox.

He also explained that I hadn't been moved from the squadron for arbitrary reasons. The regimental commander had purposely given me the job as a developmental opportunity. He knew that, in order to be competitive for a battalion command later in my career, I would need this experience, especially as a new selectee for promotion to major. My boss also explained that I had to embrace my job as an adjutant. I had to adapt to the commander's style and not the other way around. I'd been fighting it. It was my job to work with my boss's idiosyncrasies. I should be looking for opportunities to learn rather than relive my preferred role as an operations officer in a squadron. His feedback was spot on. Like a light bulb going off over my head, I understood I had to change my attitude about the job.

As a result, my performance and attitude both improved. I realized I was getting experience in, and exposure to, the workings of Army leadership that I wouldn't otherwise have had. My regimental commander was going to be a general officer, likely a four-star. He had me write correspondence for him that was meant to be read by the highest levels of the Army. For example, we were together on the inter-German border the day the wall came down, on November 9, 1989. The day was of enormous strategic consequence to the United States, given the resources we had poured into fighting the Cold War. I was privy to the conversations the commander had with both the Pentagon and the senior leadership in Europe when the border opened up. At the time, we weren't fully aware of what was happening, and we suspected some sort of Soviet ruse or attempt to infiltrate undercover soldiers into West Germany as civilians. It was high adventure those first few days and weeks, and I had a front-row seat to watch it unfold. All of which I might have missed had I not been given valuable feedback from my boss, which allowed me to turn the situation around.

Imagine if I'd been given that information right from the start. Or, if I'd been vulnerable enough to ask for feedback. It would have eliminated frustration for both the commander and me. I would have had a better understanding of the reasons I'd been assigned to the job and would have been better able to support my boss. It shouldn't take things blowing up or breaking down for feedback to be given. By that time, it can be too late.

Setting out clear expectations at the start of any job is a form of feedback. It puts everyone on the same page and sets the context for future performance discussions. It's why job descriptions are important, so people understand their accountabilities. Then, when expectations aren't met, it is a much easier conversation if this groundwork has been laid.

As mentioned earlier, there are a number of reasons that feedback is difficult and leaves people feeling exposed. It requires a level of trust between the giver and receiver. To create a feedback-friendly environment, then, it is necessary to establish trust. Remember, trust is foundational to any relationship, whether personal or professional. Like setting expectations, this must happen early in the process.

Target Corporation prides itself on being an organization that promotes ongoing and regular feedback. But when I came into the organization as the senior director of a major distribution center in Target's supply chain, I was an unknown entity. All everyone knew was I came from the Army and was a retired major general with no retail logistics or supply chain experience. None.

Since so few people in our country serve in the military anymore (less than 1% of the U.S. population), almost all of my subordinates had no hands-on experience with Army culture and its leaders. There was apprehension, hesitancy, and uncertainty about what I would be like. Did I have a sense of humor? Was I a rigid disciplinarian? A taskmaster? Whatever preconceived notions my staff had were real. Before I could expect them to provide me with honest feedback or be receptive to mine, I had to address these apprehensions and establish trust.

During the onboarding process at Target, I visited several different distribution centers, and the directors of each gave me some valuable guidance. One new peer with a lot of experience in the company told me that exhibiting behaviors that had been ingrained in me in the Army—standing with my hands on my hips or crossing my arms when talking to people, finishing people's sentences, not maintaining eye contact, asking predominantly Yes or No questions—would not help me gain footing in my new job. In Target's culture, these behaviors didn't encourage trust and were not engaging. They intimidated some people, so I needed to be mindful of how I came across.

When I returned to my own distribution center, I could see he was right. These almost-unconscious behaviors appeared to impact my interactions with others. My body language and mannerisms sometimes made others hesitant and uncertain about how to approach me. To fix it, I had to be more vulnerable. I acknowledged to my team that I'd learned or adopted certain ways of behaving in the Army and that I wanted to change them. I asked for help to do so. I requested people on my team—a subordinate or two, my HR manager, and my boss—to point out whenever they observed me demonstrating any of these behaviors, so that I could actively change and improve my effectiveness. By doing this and taking to heart the feedback they gave, I came up with an improvement plan. This allowed me to develop the necessary trust, vital to giving and receiving good feedback with my team, and it enabled me to be the engaging leader that I believe I naturally am.

In 2017, Target implemented a new program designed to break down potential trust barriers within teams and create more vulnerable leaders. They introduced it at one of our leadership gatherings in Minneapolis. It was called the *I Am From* exercise.

The idea behind it was simple. Take a piece of paper, write "I Am From" at the top, and then fill it in. Write things about yourself others wouldn't know—what makes you tick, what your biases are, what developmental experiences led you to become the person you are, what enriches you, and any other information that might provide insight—and then share it with your subordinates. The thinking was that, by doing so, by being vulnerable, leaders could let their teams know them better and understand their behavior. It would open up two-way feedback communication, establish trust, and also encourage inclusivity by shedding light on others' differing life experiences.

At this meeting, my boss shared her *I Am From* with her direct reports, about eight of us.

She was born in the United States to Muslim parents who'd immigrated from the Middle East. She talked about living in mostly all-white communities (her parents were engineers, and she had an upper-middle-class upbringing). When 9/11 happened, people began to look at her differently. What were once solid relationships became uncomfortable and weighty for her. When Donald Trump gained the presidency and unleashed anti-Muslim rhetoric and Muslim travel bans, her life again became uncomfortable, and it made her angry. She was as much of an American as any white male born and raised in small-town America by Christian parents, even if her heritage and gender meant the wider world didn't feel the same way about her. She felt isolated.

Her anger and resentment served as fuel for her to make herself the best she could be. It manifested itself in her work ethic. She was determined, almost fanatically, to do more research, work harder, and study more intensively than anyone else to overcome her feeling of isolation. She cautioned us that, because of this, she could be overbearing, work crazy hours, and expect others to do as she did. She realized she could be hard on subordinates who got things done, but not necessarily the way she did. What she wanted from us was to point out when she was in that mode so that she could modify her approach.

I found it a powerful experience. I thought a lot about how vulnerable she had to be to share her story with us. Yet, how beneficial her insight had been for her team, for those of us whose life experience had been so different!

Eventually, I put together my own *I Am From* and shared it individually with each member of my team. I asked if they'd be willing to develop something similar and share it with our entire leadership group. All agreed, and we organized an off-site meeting. It turned out to be one of the best team-building events I've ever led. Many people shared how important their faith and family were. Others took a different tack and opened up about personal setbacks, moments of grief, extreme joy, or how they ended up in their career (one gentleman had tried his hand at being an artist, for example, before deciding it wasn't going to work out and going back to school to get a degree in business).

I learned that a woman who reported to me had had two miscarriages, which was why she insisted on making it to her kids' events and occasionally working from home in the summer when they were out of school. I learned that a man's dad had abandoned his family when he was little, that he looked after a brother who was a drug addict, and that he was determined to be a great dad to his burgeoning family (five kids at last count). Another told of challenges in a relationship with someone struggling with gender identification. Another woman said she hadn't read a book in years because it was hard for her to concentrate (she had ADHD), but she loved hearing about books from others so she could participate by watching movies or series based on them.

Some of my direct reports shared more than others, but no one made the group uncomfortable by sharing too much. It brought our team closer together and helped us understand what others' preferences were, their insecurities, and what they liked or didn't. And most important, it established a higher level of trust among us so that giving and receiving feedback became easier, more specific, and more effective.

I will make a caveat here. This is not the kind of exercise that can be forced upon a group. If the entire team is not on-board and willing, it shouldn't be done. Making oneself vulnerable has to be a choice, not an edict. Everyone must see the benefit of it.

Once trust is established, leaders have an obligation and responsibility to give ongoing feedback to those working for them. It shouldn't be looked at as a once-a-year chore. All leaders should be developing and promoting the people under them, and this can't be done without providing the type of feedback that will make people grow, gain confidence, and find success.

How this is done matters tremendously. Leaders should present information in a context that says they are rooting for the people receiving the feedback. Leaders should be clear that they want their subordinates to be successful, that they want them to achieve their goals, and that they are willing to help them do so. But most of all, feedback should never be about the leader. The focus should always be on the other person.

Here are some general guidelines to follow:

Do's

1. Describe the specific behavior that needs to change, and do so without using judgment—just the facts. Using verbs rather than adjectives helps. *She didn't listen to the client's request* instead of *She was impatient.*

2. Focus on what *you noticed* about the behavior, not on what others might have said about it.

3. Be clear about the message you are delivering without vacillating, rambling, talking in vague statements, speaking on behalf of others, or muddying up the message with other tactics.

Don'ts

1. Don't judge the person. Focus on their behaviors—what they did.

2. Don't use clichés or vague phrases that leave the person wondering what the feedback refers to, such as, *You're so good.*

3. Don't sandwich negative feedback between positive statements.

4. Don't generalize with words like "always" or "never." It creates defensiveness.

5. Don't go on and on. People stop listening, and it devalues the feedback.

6. Don't make yourself a psychologist and attempt to explain someone's behavior.

7. Don't ever use feedback as a subtle threat. *If you don't get with the program . . .*

8. Don't pose feedback as a rhetorical question that suggests behavioral change is optional. *Do you think you might . . . ?*

9. Don't inject humor or use sarcasm.

10. Don't bring your own emotional baggage into the conversation.

Lists like these are useful, but let's face it, human interactions are complicated, and it is easy for good intentions to derail. During my third or fourth year with Target, a man we'll call Tom transferred to my facility. He was highly regarded in distribution and had been identified as an up-and-comer, with potential to do more. Tom wanted to relocate because he and his wife had family in the area. He said he thought we ran a good facility and wanted to be part of the team, to continue to grow and develop, and to achieve his longer-term goals. He checked all the boxes.

Once in the job, however, problems began to emerge. Although Tom was very knowledgeable about the business (he knew more about running a facility than I did), he felt the need to let everyone know it. He sniped at me and others during meetings, occasionally rolling his eyes when he didn't like an idea. He made it generally known his ideas were best, he could do my job and everyone else's better than they could, and he saw himself at a level above the rest of us. He built himself a little coalition of two of my other direct reports, who usually agreed with everything he said, pitting his group against the others. His behavior began to cause division within the team. My HR manager was as concerned as I was about the impact he was having.

Tom's behavior bothered me on several levels. First, I didn't like the influence he had on certain members of our team. Second, the way he tried to undermine me rubbed me the wrong way. It felt personal. He and another peer began to go for lunch outside the facility, extending the lunch hour, while it was established practice for the rest of my team to eat at their desks or in the cafeteria. Hourly team members couldn't leave the facility, so why should executives routinely do so? It created a bad perception. To address the issue, I put an end to people routinely going off-site for lunch unless it was a special occasion. This did not sit well with Tom and his lunch companion, but they complied. This was my first mistake. Instead of addressing the long lunches with them directly and specifically, I made a blanket policy for everybody.

When I did schedule a feedback session with Tom, I made my second mistake. I made it personal. Not long into the session, I accused him of undermining me and wanting my job. He turned to me with smugness and said, "Well, Mike, how much longer do you think you *are* going to be here?" His tone and attitude set me off, and I got angry. I told him, "You always come across as arrogant, trying to impress everyone that you're the smartest guy in the room." And the whole conversation devolved from there. We argued, and he left the room. I sat there smoldering, realizing I'd violated any number of best-practice rules—I'd made my feedback personal, got emotional, and generalized.

It's not surprising that Tom lodged a complaint with my boss. He alleged that I had it out for him, making it impossible for him to get a fair shot in the company. After investigating the situation, Target negotiated a separation with him, and Tom left the company. During the investigation, it became clear that he wasn't a good fit for the Target culture and had been problematic on the team, but my handling of the situation made the whole process more difficult for everyone.

In looking back at my behavior, I let my own insecurities at being new to the distribution game cloud my objectivity. Or maybe it was the whole alpha-male thing—being defensive when challenged. In hindsight, I could see that his combination of arrogance, inability to listen to others, and smug certainty pushed all my buttons. We're all human, and it is inevitable that at some point, most leaders will run into a Tom who gets under their skin.

But when that happens, instead of charging into a feedback session with guns blazing, smart leaders will step back, take a deep breath, and remember that, when giving feedback, objectivity and specificity are critical. The goal is to provide the other person with information that will help them improve—not to use the session as a place to vent your own feelings. Who knows? If I'd handled things better, Tom may have been able to change his behavior enough to remain a part of the team.

On another occasion, I had an opening on my team for a senior operations manager to run my warehousing department. I hired Chelsea, a woman who had been recommended by a peer of mine in Ohio. She was in her twenties and had been a rock star as an operations manager, which was an executive level below the job for which she was being considered, so it would be a major promotion. She was young for the job, but she was smart and engaging, and she had an abundance of energy.

As with the case of Tom, shortly after she began her job, problems emerged. She'd taken over an underperforming department, and instead of improving, her department's performance metrics remained sluggish. Her management style was controlling and directive; she wanted everyone in her department to do it her way. This style began to turn off the operations managers who reported to her.

As I did with all departments, I spent time on the floor engaging with her executives and team members, garnering feedback. I listened to what was on their minds and what they were saying could be done to improve things. It became apparent that her team felt their ideas weren't being heard, that they had no say in running the department, and that they were becoming less engaged. Every year, Target conducts a *Best Team Survey*, where leaders and team members take a comprehensive voluntary survey on various aspects of engagement, inclusion, development, and trust. Chelsea joined our team in January, and the survey was conducted in May. Her survey results were poor. I could see things were deteriorating.

After a couple more months of observing and assessing the situation, I sat Chelsea down and told her that her performance was subpar, that the way she led her team wasn't sustainable, and that she would need to make changes if she wanted to be successful. With her promotion, she'd taken on an operational role significantly larger than she'd had in her previous job, and she couldn't run it in the same hands-on way. Because she micromanaged her team, morale among her execs was plummeting, and her department's performance was lagging behind that of her peers. She would have to change her tactics and start leading through others.

In a nutshell, I explained to her that as a senior operations manager, she needed to elevate her game. She faced the challenge many do when moving up, especially as quickly as she had. She'd gone from operations manager directly to a senior operations manager without any intervening roles to teach her how to lead at the next level. If she couldn't master this new type of leadership, she couldn't do the job effectively. I let her know that she was highly valued, that I wanted her to succeed, and that I was willing to invest the time and effort necessary to help her do so. We came up with a program of weekly coaching from me, specific actions to undertake with her team, and an agreement on how we would measure her progress.

Over the next six months, I saw a dramatic improvement in both her leadership and business results—out-of-the-ballpark progress. She improved so much that her warehouse department rose to one of the top 5 out of 40 in the company. Before I left in August 2019, she had been promoted to a critical position at headquarters, and today, she continues to excel in positions of increased responsibility and scope.

Keep in mind that, even when done right, not all feedback yields results like Chelsea's. The point is that all of it should be done in a way that makes success like hers possible—something I didn't do for Tom. This is why becoming good at this all-important skill is vital for any organization and its growth. Growth comes out of an investment in people.

Whether giving or receiving feedback, in a conducive environment or not, the same rules apply. The end goal is to produce positive forward movement that will benefit all involved. Feedback should not be a once-a-year thing; it should be a regular part of the organizational culture. It shouldn't be solely results-focused, either. When performance suffers, there are likely certain behaviors that have contributed to less-than-satisfactory results. Change won't happen unless those behaviors are addressed. But above all, feedback should be objective and specific, and it should be given empathetically.

Giving and receiving feedback is a skill that demands vulnerability on both sides. I urge you to make a practice of it. Remember, the more you work a muscle, the more limber it becomes. The same goes for feedback. Even seasoned leaders sometimes get it wrong, but making mistakes can be useful if lessons are learned.

And practice makes perfect.

‹ ‹ ◆ › ›

– 11 –

LEADING THROUGH OTHERS

Vulnerable leaders enable others
and leave a human legacy

What is one of the most common workplace complaints? According to a LinkedIn survey, 79% of employees say they had a micromanaging boss at some point in their career. These are bosses who want to control their work environment down to the minutest detail. I certainly understand the urge. Who wouldn't want everything done exactly to their own preference?

But being a good leader is not about controlling minutiae. It's about providing your team with an objective and giving them the freedom to find a way to meet it. It means telling someone what needs to be done but not how to do it, trusting others to do the job.

Without a doubt, giving up the reins can feel risky and make bosses feel vulnerable. But that is exactly what good leaders should strive for—getting comfortable with a level of uncertainty. They should throw aside the old adage, *If you want something done right, do it yourself,* and empower others to take the helm, even when it means giving up some control.

It's not surprising that many leaders are promoted because they're top performers. The idea that, if they excel in one job they're likely to excel in another, sounds reasonable. But leadership skills are not the same as technical skills or on-the-job expertise. Being good at one does not guarantee you will be good at the other. And as the scope of responsibility in a job increases, the less technical skills matter and the more leadership abilities do. To be able to lead effectively through others, a leader must learn how to give up the hands-on control that is intertwined with technical skills. And that requires vulnerability.

In the Army, lieutenants start out leading a platoon of around 20 to 40 soldiers, depending on the branch—infantry, armor, engineer, or sustainment, for example. They progress to becoming a captain commanding a company of roughly 60 to 150 soldiers, and then a lieutenant colonel, commanding a battalion of anywhere from 300 to 700 soldiers, followed by a colonel, leading a brigade of 1,500 to 5,000 soldiers. Although all echelons except platoon have subordinate officers that help lead the soldiers under their care, you can see that the scope of responsibility vastly increases the farther up the chain of command one travels. Lieutenants can easily be involved in all aspects of the platoon's work and intimately familiar with each soldier in their command, and they should be. That becomes impossible by the time an officer becomes a colonel and takes command of a brigade.

I became acutely aware of this when I went from a lieutenant colonel commanding a battalion to a colonel commanding a brigade. As a battalion commander, I was responsible for roughly 500 troops and their officers, in addition to a dedicated staff—personnel, intelligence, operations, logistics, air defense, and signal. At this level of command, it's still possible to reach out and connect with soldiers and interact with them routinely enough to exert a direct influence.

But when I moved up to command a brigade at Fort Riley, Kansas, which numbered about 5,000, including officers, that was not the case. Although I had similar staff support—of higher rank and more experience—the job I was doing was vastly different in numbers as well as purpose and accountability. It meant I had to shift my mode of leading.

Before I took command of the brigade, though, I was lucky enough to receive coaching about what this leadership shift might entail. While in Bosnia-Herzegovina in 1998–1999 as part of a multinational force, I'd been selected for promotion to colonel and then a few months later for command of a brigade. Although I wouldn't pin on my new rank for another 18 months, I was fortunate that a brigadier general in our division in Bosnia, the Assistant Division Commander (ADC), took an active interest in me. He mentored me and helped me understand how I'd have to change my leadership style when it came time for me to take over brigade command.

A gentle man with a kind face and eyes that lit up when he smiled, the ADC had an avuncular way about him. He was thoughtful and intelligent. I met him first when I was a major attending the School for Advanced Military Studies at Fort Leavenworth, a rigorous academic year focused on studying war. He was a senior fellow there at the time and wrote a brilliant monograph that made us all think he was a god. Working with him again in Bosnia just added to my respect for him.

He wasn't required to mentor me. But he did. After learning about my selection, he set up a series of appointments before he had to rotate out of his role and move onto another stateside position. Over the next couple of months, we met and discussed the leadership challenges that would face me a year later.

Our headquarters were at the Tuzla airbase in Bosnia. It was an old Soviet base when Bosnia-Herzegovina had been part of Yugoslavia. The command's staff offices were in a typically drab building, dressed in graying white stucco with a red-clay-tiled roof and no visible adornment. Inside, dreary pale-green walls, poor lighting, and cheap linoleum hearkened back to the days of the Cold War. In the evening, about once a week, we'd meet in his office—a spacious but spartan room—a desk, chairs, and sitting area—and not much else.

Normally, he'd usher me in, and we'd take our place in his sitting area. "Mike," he'd begin, "leading at the next level is all about intent."

He knew that only a few years separated giving up command of a battalion and taking command of a brigade (three years in my case). The comfortable thing for many is to continue a hands-on approach and lead by doing. And while many brigade commanders do exactly that, he suggested the best didn't.

In his mind, a brigade commander's main job was to let his intent be known to his subordinates, and then allow them to figure out the details necessary to achieve it. By "intent," he meant that a brigade commander should clearly let his battalion commanders know the purpose of the mission at hand, the key tasks required for it to occur, and the end results expected or what success would look like. He believed this notion of intent is what leadership is about at all but the lowest tactical levels. And that it becomes increasingly more important the higher up the chain of command one goes.

He leaned over, his thinning gray hair framing his earnest face. "In fact, nearly everything you do as a brigade commander should be intent-based."

Over the course of our meetings, he laid out the things I needed to focus on to become a master of intentionality. First, in speaking my intent, I should include not only my purpose, key tasks, and expected results but also the right and left boundaries—guidelines broad enough for my subordinates to maneuver within—to help them make informed decisions. Things like what resources were available, what the time frame was, any known land mines that needed to be circumvented, and how often progress reports were expected—all the information they needed to ensure their success. Then I should step back and let them go to it, periodically checking their progress, stepping in only to course-correct if things weren't working. In other words, give them the framework, and let them build the house.

Second, I should allow my subordinates into my head and let them see how I liked to operate, what I found important, and how my mind worked so that there would be fewer chances for them to misunderstand my intent. Be an open book and not a cipher.

Third, after accomplishing our assigned missions, my next priority should be developing my subordinates and setting them up for success as future brigade commanders or other positions of increased responsibility. Leadership development is critical for the Army, and it should be critical for any organization that wants to thrive. He told me that, at all times, I should be able to answer the question, *If something happened to me, who would take over until a permanent replacement could be found, and have I done what I could to make that person succeed?*

Leading by intent means forcing subordinates to think for themselves and not giving them all the answers. That is the best way to develop them for the future.

Fourth, a brigade commander should push decision-making down the chain of command as far as possible. This helps develop subordinates at every level, even if mistakes are made. That's how people learn. Commanders who want to ensure things are done perfectly to their specifications, who have to approve every communication down to the exact wording, do nothing to create the next generation of leaders.

"I can't stress developing people enough," he said. "Once, as a brigade commander, I needed a major within my brigade to take over as my operations officer. Instead of selecting the one I thought best, I asked all my battalion commanders to get together. I said, 'Each of you has two majors. I need all of you to figure out which one is the best to replace my operations officer.' I told them what abilities I was looking for and made sure they knew what the responsibilities of the job were. I gave them an hour to figure it out." He gave me a little grin. "And damned if they didn't come back with a recommendation for the very same officer I would have picked." He was adamant that asking for this level of input and decision-making is the surest way to develop independent-thinking future leaders.

Finally, he imparted to me that the brigade commander sets the tone. No matter what the mission is, whether it's distasteful or routine, a good leader sends the message to his troops that they must and will do it to the very best of their ability. Whether it's as mundane as cutting the grass on the post or picking up trash in public areas, it must be undertaken with the same level of commitment to excellence as any combat mission. The brigade commander makes it a matter of pride and motivates the team to want to excel despite the nature of the work they're doing. That, the general concluded, is truly the art of leadership.

The last thing he shared with me was how he had occasionally screwed things up, by acting not quite in alignment with what he was telling me. He freely admitted instances he'd go back and do differently. But he also pointed out that these setbacks, these moments he would like to change, were the moments where he'd learned the most. He said I should realize that not everything will play out as I would like.

"Don't fear failure, Mike. Rather, when it happens—because it will—your job is to ensure maximum learning for you and your team. Everyone wants things to go according to plan, but that is, indeed, a rare occurrence. Plan on it."

It's tough to express how grateful I was to my assistant division commander for the time he spent with me. He was one of those rare individuals who modeled what he preached. His video matched his audio. His words stuck with me when I took over brigade command at Fort Riley a year later. I endeavored to lead by intent the way he'd laid it out for me. I like to think that I was successful. To make clear my intent, I had to give my subordinates what they needed to move forward and then let them do the work without interference. His words gave me the confidence to give up tight control and focus on empowering and developing those who reported to me.

Sadly, not everyone is provided the coaching I received. I saw many un-empowering leaders in the Army—both peers and bosses. As I was settling into what I thought would be my second year in the Pentagon, out of the blue I was notified that I was being reassigned to another major Army installation. There, my new job entailed playing two distinct roles on the Army post. One was the senior mission commander, who certified that all deploying units were trained and ready to go. The second was as the assistant division commander of a combat division of about 25,000 soldiers.

The challenge I faced was that, except for a brigade combat team located with me, the rest of my division was based elsewhere. The division was split unevenly between the two locations, with my two-star boss along with most of the rest of the division living and working in another state. That meant that, as one of two assistant division commanders—the other was based with the bulk of the troops—I was the sole senior officer at my installation representing the division.

For that reason, I was tasked with interacting with local community officials and the installation commander (another two-star, who was not thrilled that I showed up as the senior mission commander, taking over a role he'd been executing for the past year). I had to juggle the desires of both generals—my long-distance boss in another state and the installation commander on my post. It didn't help that my two-star boss had a controlling leadership style.

Summer was approaching, and another brigade combat team was relocating to my installation as part of the eventual move of the entire division over the next several years. This was a big deal for any Army post. Having 5,000 soldiers with their families join the local community meant more housing needs both on and off post, more money siphoned into the local economy, and the expansion of on-post resources in anticipation of the new arrivals. In other words, an economic benefit all around, great public relations for the Army, and a source of pride for the local community.

For the event, I intended to hold a big ceremony to welcome the brigade to its new home. I planned to invite local officials and dignitaries and showcase our troops to the community. I informed my division commander's staff of my intentions and mentioned the event to my boss several times. He didn't seem that interested, but receiving no objections, I proceeded to plan the ceremony. It should be noted that military ceremonies are big affairs and involve a lot of preparation and coordination in advance.

About a week before the big day, my boss called me in a huff about the event. It surprised me since he'd said nothing about it until this call. I explained the details, including the arrangements we'd made, who was coming, and what a great reception we expected. He barely listened. He insisted I cancel the ceremony because he couldn't personally be there. While he had planned on coming, a conflict arose, and he was adamant that no ceremony involving one of his brigades could go forward without him. "I'm the face of the division," he said, "and you'll have to move it to a time when I can attend." He ordered me to reschedule the event.

Shocked by his disregard for the disruption and chaos this sudden change would cause, I told him it would be an embarrassment for the division. The invitations had gone out, RSVPs received, and schedules cleared. The ceremony had been on the calendar for a couple of months. We would look like amateurs. Still, he wouldn't back down. I asked him to think about what he was asking and the headaches it would cause for his team. Not to mention that summers at Army installations are ceremony-heavy—most changes of command happened during that season, when kids were out of school, to minimize disruption to already chaotic lives. Plus, with units deploying and returning from combat, it was a busy time of year for departure and welcome-home ceremonies. It wasn't a simple thing to reschedule an event like the one I'd planned. He refused to change his mind and ended the phone conversation upset that I had even questioned him.

I quickly dialed my wingman, my fellow assistant division commander. "What the hell is with him?" I asked and explained the situation. My friend had no clue. I asked if he would try to reason with our boss face to face and try to get him to see the issues with his order. Instantly grasping the problem, my friend said he'd do what he could. I waited on eggshells, canceling nothing, knowing that if my boss didn't change his mind, and I went ahead with the ceremony without him, I'd be in hot water.

A couple of days later, my boss called back and begrudgingly told me to go ahead with the ceremony. He made it clear he wasn't happy. In a gruff tone, he added that he would tolerate no more undermining from me. He was the commander of the division, and I had to do a better job of coordinating my activities with the rest of the division.

The ceremony proceeded as planned and proved to be a fitting day for such a significant event for the local community. A lot of goodwill was garnered that day. Little benefit came out of it, however, for my relationship with my boss. He couldn't see that my actions had nothing to do with him or that my motivation was only for the division and the local community. All he could see was that his control and position had been questioned. If, in fact, the problem had been that I had not sufficiently coordinated the event, he missed a moment to coach me. He made it clear to me that what he expected was for his subordinates to obey without question.

Unfortunately, this was not an isolated incident. I saw other instances of the same kind of obsessive control and lack of empowerment manifest themselves at other times within the division. I learned little from the man except how to placate him until one of us moved on.

This is not unique to the Army. I saw the same urge to control with several of my peers at Target when senior management visited our facilities. My boss and others from headquarters would periodically tour our facilities with an agenda designed to inform them about each operation. They wanted to learn about our successes and challenges, help with things we needed, interview prospective candidates for promotion, and interface with our entire teams. On such visits, I rarely did much talking. I doled out subject areas or issues to my team that my boss wanted to dive into during the visit, and I let them do most of the talking. To begin with, my team members were the experts on the issues, not me. Second, I saw it as a developmental opportunity. How were they ever going to get comfortable presenting information to upper leadership, including proposing solutions and approaches, if I did all the talking whenever a bigwig showed up?

I always ensured beforehand they were prepared. We rehearsed until they felt ready. Not only was it great for their professional and personal confidence, but it gave me an opportunity to provide coaching to them, much as my ADC in Bosnia did, when mistakes were made. And, it was a huge hit with my boss—she saw what I was doing and fully endorsed it. She understood that leaders who empower must provide these kinds of opportunities so that their people learn from experience. That it was beneficial to allow our folks the latitude to do things their way within established guidelines. And, that when honest mistakes occur, we should underwrite them.

I didn't always see the same thing when I was invited to go along on these visits to other facilities. Often my peers would do most of the talking, answering other people's questions for them, and playing the role of being "large and in charge" at their facility. The other thing I rarely heard uttered were the words "I don't know." It was clear some of my peers didn't want anyone to believe they didn't have a firm handle on all aspects of their business. Because of this, they sometimes got themselves in trouble from a credibility standpoint, giving incomplete or inaccurate information in response to questions tossed their way. Simply saying *I don't know, but I'll get back to you with the answer* would have been so much better.

I don't have any data on how my peers who exercised tight control over their operations and subordinates fared. But I can say the most successful ones I worked with were those who felt comfortable allowing their people to interface with headquarters' leadership. I took great pride in showcasing my team. Why wouldn't I? Much like successful children of good parents, didn't my staff reflect the investment I personally made in their development? I can proudly say that three of my former direct reports are now senior directors for Target.

So, we're back to the main question. If 79% of people have experienced a boss like mine, who wanted to cancel the Army ceremony, or like some of my peers at Target, why does this continue to be such a pervasive problem for people when they move into a leadership position? Wouldn't people who have experienced a hands-on boss strive to be different?

Maybe people who have been micromanaged their entire careers and then ascend into leadership don't know how to do it any other way. Maybe not everyone is given the coaching I received. Maybe they don't know how to put the coaching they receive into practice. All of which may be true. But I suspect the main reason is that when people are uncomfortable in a new role, rather than appearing not to know how to do their new jobs, they default to micromanaging—hoping to maintain control by in-the-weeds oversight of their subordinates. They want to be the expert, exude competence and confidence, and show they have mastery over their domain at all times. They don't want to show any vulnerability.

Today, we are awash in technology that brings data instantly to our fingertips, and that makes micromanaging even more tempting. Leaders now have access to information at the moment it happens, even at echelons far below them. Instead of focusing on higher-level tasks, they can spend hours sifting through data, analyzing it, and second-guessing the decisions of the people they have hired to do that work. The old saying, *Just because you can, doesn't mean you should,* is an apt one.

Recently, I've done some consulting with the Army's Leader Training Program, developed to help brigade commanders understand what effective leadership looks like at their level in today's Army, especially given the current strategic situation facing the United States. The Army realized that, having spent the last 20 years focusing on counterinsurgency operations in Iraq and Afghanistan, it must now pivot to be prepared for the possibility of large-scale combat operations in the event of war with forces from Russia or China. That preparation starts with training leaders and their staff to be able to plan for and execute such major operations.

When you're dealing with terrorists, there is no need to maneuver large formations like brigades on the ground or to coordinate artillery support, naval and air power, and support functions such as supply, engineer, and signal on a large scale. Rather, what's needed are small-unit operations—think about the commando unit that took down Osama bin Laden—with a small, finite scope of control. This means that during the last 20 years of counterinsurgency, many commanders now commanding battalions and brigades progressed through the ranks as lieutenants, captains, and majors, knowing little else beyond these smaller operations. They didn't have to think about the challenges associated with maneuvering brigades and divisions in more conventional ways—to attack and defend. Obviously, the level of coordination and synchronization is vastly more complicated the bigger the operation gets.

What today's battalion and brigade leaders did experience as they led small units focused on counterinsurgency was a greater degree of scrutiny and control from *their* leadership, enabled by today's technology. That level of involvement and control is all they knew. They grew accustomed to micromanagement and second-guessing—the antithesis of leading through others. It's not surprising that, in many cases, that's how they command today, even though that style of leadership doesn't work with large-scale operations. Immersing themselves in the minutest details at several levels below their level of responsibility doesn't serve them well for what lies ahead.

For this reason, the Leadership Training Program was designed to help commanders re-learn broader leadership skills that have atrophied over the last 20 years. I was asked to help coach brigade commanders in this vein. Specifically, these colonels needed to be retrained on how to lead in the fashion that my ADC in Bosnia taught me, how to be intent-based leaders and effective with a wider scope of responsibility.

Not surprisingly, I found that many of the commanders I worked with had a strong tendency to want to control everything, with a penchant for details far below their position and a thirst for data that quickly overwhelmed them. An overabundance of information kept them from paying attention to the bigger picture, focusing on what lay beyond the horizon, and anticipating their next crucial steps—all skills that are critical to leading troops in large-scale operations.

In coaching these commanders, I also found that some were open to change, and others were not. Those who were open admitted they were rusty, having not led or conducted planning exercises for large combat situations recently, if ever. They accepted feedback gratefully from all sources and encouraged input from their staff. Their focus was preparing not only themselves but also their teams to be ready to take on future missions that would likely be very different from what they'd been doing. They accepted that they didn't know all the answers. They allowed themselves to be vulnerable. They understood that doing so would benefit not only themselves but their unit and the Army as a whole.

Those who weren't open didn't want to admit they needed to re-learn any skills. They felt that after 20-plus years in the Army and having achieved the highly respected and selective rank of colonel, it was beneath them to go back to the basics and fundamentals of leading a brigade. They often ignored or discounted input from their staff and others, defaulting to what they knew best. In doing so, they rendered themselves and their teams far less effective.

Now, ask yourself. If you had to follow one of these commanders into a combat situation, which would you choose?

Having said all that, we live in a difficult time. Leaders at all levels are being bombarded with mixed messages about leadership, especially those at high levels. In today's hyper-driven, sensationalized news cycles, senior leaders are expected to be aware of and on top of every incident that occurs beneath them. Events can go viral immediately. Saying, "I don't know about that, but I'll look into it," often isn't enough. Headlines and social media scream for accountability and blame immediately, and the possibility of losing a job becomes real.

Today's senior noncommissioned officers—first sergeants and command sergeants major—are required to have social media accounts and be instantaneously responsive to negative postings by soldiers regarding everything from the quality of food in the dining facilities to housing problems to harassment from superiors. Day or night, they must be on top of it. The same is true in many corporations.

At Target, it was understood by many senior leaders that all executives should respond to texts and emails outside of work in a timely manner, especially once a batch of outside executives was brought on board and put into senior leadership positions. These highly talented people were hired to help Target revamp and improve its e-commerce business, and they did. But they also came from a culture where this around-the-clock availability, constant immersion in the business, and data-always-available mentality was the norm. My boss began to contact me occasionally at night if her boss asked her about some issue. I pushed back because it was exhausting and displayed a lack of trust. I told her that, after nine at night, I was not looking at my phone until the next morning. I was firm, and she relented. (Sometimes she'd go around me directly to one of my direct reports, which infuriated me, but that's another story.)

Because of the 24-hour nature of today's media, leaders are being told that nothing can wait—everything must be addressed immediately. All of which send the message that micromanaging is acceptable. It implies that good leaders should have their hands on every detail of the business.

But society sends us many messages about how we should live our lives. That doesn't mean we should listen. While I'm not suggesting you ignore the real demands that technology and social media place on leaders, I am suggesting that you do not let it consume you. Or drive you to a controlling style of leadership. Data, technology, and social media are just part of work these days. They must be managed like any other aspect of a leader's job, even if they're troublesome or problematic at times.

The Army has a saying about moving up the chain of command. "The higher up the flagpole you ascend, the more your ass shows"—the more exposed you are, the more vulnerable. There you are with it all hanging out. But that is the nature of leadership. When you take on a leadership position, you agree to take responsibility for all that happens on your watch. Whether you like it or not, you have put yourself in a vulnerable position.

Once you've said "Yes" to that responsibility, you have two choices. Either you can try to control everything that happens, or you can enlist others to help you meet your goals by leading through them. The two options will not produce the same results. The first option will always be limited because you have a finite amount of time and attention. There's no way around it.

However, if you choose the second option and devote your finite time and attention to working through others to help achieve your goals, it takes the question of limits off the table. Your chances of success soar, and you have the added bonus of leaving a legacy through the people you've developed to take your place.

All it takes to choose option two is understanding the inherent vulnerability of being a leader, embracing it, and making it your partner.

◂ ◂ ◆ ▸ ▸

– 12 –

CARING LEADERSHIP

*Vulnerability enables empathy,
the catalyst for caring*

Like everything else, the demands on leaders have evolved over the centuries, even if intrinsic leadership qualities haven't. What this means is that to accomplish the same results, people managing organizations have had to change not only their focus but also their behaviors.

In her article "Management's Three Eras: A Brief History," published in the *Harvard Business Review* in 2014, Rita McGrath wrote, "I'd propose that we've seen three "ages" of management since the industrial revolution, with each putting the emphasis on a different theme: execution, expertise, and empathy."

Looking first at the industrial revolution, she points out that, with the advent of new technologies, goods could be produced in greater quantity and scale through mass production. This required a whole new way of organizing a business. No longer was one person making a product from beginning to end. Instead, a group of people working together churned out an end product at a faster rate. This required someone to oversee the work process, determine how to divide up labor, establish a means of quality control, and implement a different way of accounting. To accomplish this, the focus of company leaders shifted almost solely to the execution or process of the work needed to produce optimum output.

In the mid-twentieth century, with the advent of computers and software, another shift occurred. This time the focus moved from product manufacturing to providing services. Management gurus like Peter Drucker saw that value was created not only by executing tasks but also by using information. He called it "knowledge work." As this type of nonproduction work increased in a new service economy, an employee was no longer just an interchangeable part in the production process. When an experienced employee left, knowledge walked out the door. Company leaders looked for ways to retain expertise, and their emphasis moved from overseeing execution to motivating and engaging employees, who had become knowledge assets.

Today we are looking at another shift of focus within organizations. With increased information-sharing and connectivity, no longer is execution or expertise enough. It is now important to provide a complete and meaningful experience to the customer. And to do that, empathy is required on several levels. Not only must empathy be shown to the customer—how else is it possible to deliver something meaningful?—but also to the employees who must make the experience happen. Leaders must move away from hierarchical structures and develop work communities—which can't be done without an emphasis on empathy or putting oneself in another person's shoes.

Empathy can't exist without vulnerability. In order to feel what other people feel, we need to understand what it's like to be them. We have to be willing to expose ourselves to uncomfortable emotions. We have to be in touch with our own experiences to relate to others and make a connection. We have to be willing not only to listen closely but also to authentically share our understanding and compassion with others.

Making this shift is a tall order today for many organizations still rooted in the ideas of the past and focused on execution and expertise. More than ever, this new paradigm shift requires leaders to bring empathy to the workplace. They must care. As Theodore Roosevelt famously said, "People don't care how much you know—until they know how much you care."

So, what does this new kind of empathetic leader look like?

In an ideal world, a caring leader shows concern for the well-being of others over and above their personal agenda or the agenda of the organization. They listen, show empathy and compassion, treat others fairly, encourage professional and personal development, and acknowledge others. They create an environment of trust and inclusivity that builds a community around the work being done.

Sounds a lot like the kind of vulnerable leader we've talked about throughout this book, doesn't it?

When it comes to showing others they care, leaders' actions and words must match. How many times have employees heard, "My door is always open," only to find it isn't? Or been told, "I'd like honest feedback," only to find how punishing honesty can be? Or been docked for taking time off to handle a personal matter after having been assured that "you're more than an employee; you're part of our family"? Caring leadership means companies can no longer merely talk about caring; they must show it as well. And this is not always as easy as it sounds.

The Army is a unique organization in that when you join the Army, so do your spouse and your family. If your assignment puts you on an Army base, you live and work among each other in a tightly-knit community. Every two to four years, you move and start all over with another set of neighbors and colleagues. To show that the Army cares, not only about the service member but also their family, a culture and various programs have been developed to show just how valuable family support is to the Army.

Over more than a hundred years, certain structures have been put in place to assist the Army communities that have formed around military work, including providing assistance to family members. Within each various unit, camaraderie and support are created through symbols, traditions, ceremonies, and rituals that are similar across assignments. For spouses, organized social groups have been established consistently on every post—officer and noncommissioned officer wives' clubs, unit coffees, Army community-service programs, and support groups. Programs have been set up to help with spousal education and employment. For children, schools have been established on base where every student shares a common experience. On-post childcare assistance is available. Comprehensive healthcare is provided within each community, and commissaries and exchanges sell discounted food and goods.

The word "soldier" is capitalized in Army correspondence to show the importance of fighting personnel to make their families proud. Spouses are routinely acknowledged during ceremonies, thanked, and presented with plaques and awards for their support, all designed to highlight their importance to the Army. The concept of family and marriage is openly spoken about as a bedrock of Army values.

As times have changed, these structures have been modified to keep up—no longer is it assumed that all soldiers are male or that spouses don't work outside the home (although some people feel these modifications have lagged behind the broader culture). On the surface, it looks like the Army is miles ahead of others in establishing communities around the work being done. The leadership is saying all the right things.

Yet, ask soldiers about Army life and its impact on their families, and they'll tell you, "It's tough," or "It's taken a toll." Ask military spouses whether they feel like an integral part of the Army, and they're likely to say, "Sure, as long as what I'm doing benefits the Army." The truth is the military lifestyle continues to be hard on spouses and children, and the numbers show it.

Out of 21 occupations, the military has the highest divorce rate, according to research done by the career website Zippia.

Although military spouses have the same desire for employment outside the home as the wider population, they are often frustrated in attaining it. The White House Council of Economic Advisors released a report on *Military Spouses in the Labor Market* in May 2018. It reported that, even though military spouses were more highly educated than other civilian, non-institutionalized Americans of working age, they were 19% less likely to find work. In addition, employed military spouses earned 26.8% less than their civilian counterparts and were more likely to be disadvantaged by occupational licensing requirements.

The reasons for the differences between military spouses and their civilian counterparts are directly linked to the military lifestyle. Active-duty service members often have long or disruptive hours and frequent absences from home, putting the burden of parenting on the spouse. They become temporary single parents during deployments. Because of this, childcare and its expense become a larger issue for the military spouse. In addition, military families move often and, as many of the bases are in rural areas with fewer employment opportunities, spouses are more likely not to find a job in the field for which they've studied or trained. Often, they have to take entry-level jobs and start over every few years. Because every state has different occupational-licensing laws, it is difficult to maintain the required licensing and certification for many jobs.

Another area of growing concern is mental health for the entire family—service members, spouses, and children. The nature of the military lifestyle means that military families are more likely to experience Post Traumatic Stress Disorder (PTSD), anxiety, depression, marital/relationship issues, and sleep issues. Suicide rates continue to alarm.

While the Army has put in place programs to address many of these problems, they have not kept pace with the demand or changes in the marketplace. Often there are restrictions on eligibility for aid, almost insurmountable administrative and bureaucratic hurdles, waiting lists, unspoken social pressure, and a lack of consistent funding for the programs offered. There is a severe shortage of mental health professionals in many areas.

All this means that the Army has not been able to significantly impact or solve some of the issues facing military families, even while proclaiming how much they care about them. This is evident by the fact that when the above statistics about military spouses in the labor market were released in 2018, they had not significantly changed over the previous 15 years, and the inadequacy of mental-health care is consistently a top issue year after year. Increasingly, the inability to address these concerns is seen as a lack of caring and empathy on the Army's part, and it is impacting both recruiting rates and lengths of stay in the Army.

I know my wife and children encountered some of these frustrations during my time in the Army. My wife, Kim, and I were married for 28 years of my 33-year Army career, and we moved 21 times. When we entered the Army as a couple, Kim was a registered dietitian with a master's degree in nutrition and happily employed in Washington, DC, where she found a rewarding job in her field as a pediatric dietitian, working at Children's Hospital with some of the top experts in the country.

When we moved to Fulda, Germany, a very different situation faced Kim. None of her certifications were valid in a foreign country. She didn't speak the language. Her choice of jobs was limited to what the Army base had to offer. She ended up getting a job proctoring aptitude tests in the Army Education Center on our small post, which was called Downs Barracks. She was grossly overqualified and found the job tedious and boring. But it was important for her to work. My job took me out into the field for training exercises, sometimes for months at a time, and she wanted to keep busy.

Still, day after monotonous day, it hit her how much she'd given up to follow my career. In a letter to her sister, she wrote, "I had to temporarily give up my career because of my husband's, and it is really taking all my energy to not be bitter about it." It wasn't only the job that drove home this reality. Everything about life as a military spouse sent messages that her concerns and desires were secondary to the Army and her husband's career.

At one point in Germany, Kim was substitute-teaching at the high school on post. One day, she had to get home quickly after school for a meeting. Downs Barracks had only a few main roads that were less than a couple miles long, with ridiculous speed limits of 15 to 20 miles an hour. In her haste, she drove over the speed limit, going maybe 30 miles an hour. A military police officer pulled her over.

With the overblown officiousness of small-town traffic cops, he motioned for her to roll down the window. "Do you know how fast you were going, ma'am?"

My wife sheepishly admitted she'd been speeding.

"Can I see your license?"

She handed it over. He took his time examining it and then copied her information on a notepad before handing the license back. With a slight bend, he made eye contact through the open window. "Who's your sponsor, ma'am?"

At the time, military family members were considered dependents and needed to have a sponsor to receive military benefits, or in the case of overseas assignments, to live on overseas posts.

She gave him information about me. He recorded my name, put a hand on the roof of our car, and squinted at the road in front of the car.

"What's going to happen now," he told my wife, "is your husband's commanding officer will be notified about this incident. As your sponsor, your husband will be held accountable for your improper behavior. You might consider that before you speed again."

Kim drove off, stunned. She hadn't been spoken to like a second-class citizen since being a minor under her parents' care.

My commanding officer handled the whole matter as a joke, ribbing me that I needed to get control of my speed-demon wife. But I'll never forget Kim coming home and telling me how humiliated she'd been. A competent, grown woman, more than capable of taking care of herself, she'd been treated like an adolescent just because she'd married an officer and agreed to move overseas with him. She didn't understand why she couldn't just pay a fine like any other adult.

The message this small incident sent to her was *You don't matter except as an appendage of your husband.* Imagine how these seemingly small, insidious messages add up over time. Although the Army has changed this verbiage—they no longer use the word "dependents"—the impact hasn't changed. Even today, for any service used on post, the first question a spouse is asked is, "What's your sponsor's last four?" (the last four digits of their Social Security number). Most army spouses may not remember their own Social Security number, but they know their soldier's.

When we returned to the States, Kim thought things would be better. But she soon realized that her career goals and her plan to get a PhD would have to be postponed indefinitely. As we moved around and my career blossomed, we lived on Army posts adjacent to small towns such as Leavenworth, Kansas, Junction City, Kansas, Radcliff, Kentucky, and Hinesville, Georgia. By then, we had two young boys. None of these small towns offered the kind of work that had so inspired her at Children's Hospital in Washington, DC. Taking a mindless, low-paying job that wasn't satisfying didn't seem worth paying for childcare and leaving our children behind. During our boys' toddler years, she didn't even bother trying to find a job.

Nor did my wife realize her goal of attaining her PhD. None of these small towns had universities with doctoral programs, especially in her field. And even if they had, she couldn't commit to attending them for more than one or two consecutive years.

When we were at Fort Riley in Kansas and the boys were in school, she worked as a part-time dietitian at the hospital in Manhattan, Kansas, and managed to do some pediatric consulting work for Children's Mercy Hospital in Kansas City. Her desire would have been to work there full-time, but Kansas City was a two-hour drive each way. I was absent for long stretches, and a full-time job wouldn't have been feasible with two school-aged boys to care for. She was lucky to get the part-time job. Often when Army wives apply for jobs, employers take one look at their resumés and work history and dismiss them, assuming that a series of one- to two-year jobs or being married to a service member means they won't be around for long.

Like many professions, being a dietitian meant Kim had to keep up to date on continuing education and stay current on the latest research in her field. It's nearly impossible to take 20 years off from any career and expect to be qualified for open positions when you step back into the workforce.

For this reason, Kim did what she could to keep her hand in her field. Without having access to jobs where she could practice and work on her areas of interest, she ended up finding creative ways to volunteer. In Germany, she provided nutritional counseling to the Boeselager team before their 1988 competition (the Boeselager Cup was a biannual armored reconnaissance competition among NATO countries). She gave periodic talks to wives' groups and soldiers about diet, weight loss, and athletic performance at multiple duty stations. At Fort Hood in Texas, she volunteered to evaluate Army daycare and home-daycare centers for compliance with FDA nutritional standards. When

I deployed to Iraq, she developed a wellness-and-nutrition program for the spouses left behind. Later at Fort Jackson in South Carolina, she created and implemented a program to increase fruit and vegetable intake in second-graders at Army schools that caught the attention of First Lady Michelle Obama.

Of course, she had to create these opportunities for herself and wasn't paid for her expertise.

Not until our sons were in high school and we were back in Washington, DC, was Kim able to return to work as a full-time pediatric dietitian, once again at Children's Hospital. We lived in Northern Virginia, and she had at least an hour-long commute both ways. During part of our stay in DC, I was deployed. So, in addition to her full-time job, she had to raise our two teenage sons by herself. I talked earlier in the book about the strain my deployment put on her at this time. Our older son's grades dropped, and he and his friends got into trouble, bringing the police to our door multiple times. He almost ruined his chances of getting into a four-year college. All of this weighed heavily on my wife. She questioned whether her desire to work was selfish and whether she should quit her job and devote herself to getting our sons through high school. She second-guessed herself and wondered if she was a bad mother.

Then I returned from deployment and added to her burden. It was only her unbelievable resilience and emotional strength that enabled her to work through all of this and ensure that our family came out intact. Not all military families are as lucky.

After that, things started to settle down for us in DC—I'd been working as the Director of Training for the Army staff in the Pentagon for a year, and I'd been asked to stay on for another year in the same capacity. My wife was finally able to enjoy her job; our son Nick had just gone off to college in Florida, and our son Tony began his sophomore year in high school. Everyone was on-board to stay another year in DC. Then out of the blue, I was notified that I was being reassigned to Fort Carson in Colorado.

As you can imagine, our son Tony wasn't happy to leave his friends behind and finish his last few years of high school in an unknown school. And once again, my wife put her career on pause for mine. The Army needed us elsewhere. Off we went to Colorado.

Once there, Kim managed to get a full-time job as a general nutritionist at the Army hospital at Fort Carson. Granted, it was a job in her field, but not in the more challenging discipline of pediatric dietetics. It also meant another deployment where she would, again, be parenting alone, trying to get our second son through his last years in high school by herself. Dealing, yet again, with a surly adolescent, disgruntled that he'd been uprooted. The only blessing was that she didn't have a two-hour daily commute and could be at home more than she'd been with our older son.

I should mention that, along with working and raising our children, throughout all of our moves, Kim also took on the duties expected of an officer's wife. Being an Army wife is one of those thankless, unpaid jobs, especially when troops are deployed. At every level, from company up to installation command, the commander is responsible for choosing someone to run the Family Readiness Group (FRG) for their command. The FRG is an informal structure that keeps spouses and families informed and supported. Traditionally, this role falls to the commanding officer's spouse. While not required, there is often a lot of pressure for spouses to accept these responsibilities—call it an unwritten expectation.

When they do agree to play this role, they must run regular meetings, write or assign someone to create a newsletter, maintain a roster, arrange unit functions, provide support when casualties occur, and handle any other required tasks. Some of these, especially dealing with casualties, can be very emotionally draining. In addition to FRG duties, spouses are expected to coordinate rank-specific groups within a unit at all levels—such as the more social officer wives' coffee groups. Kim took on these responsibilities, in addition to her full-time job and parenting duties.

It wasn't until I left the Army, after 28 years of marriage, that my wife was able to go back to school and begin her PhD program, at the age of fifty-eight. Today, with doctorate in hand, she has the career she dreamt about so many years ago. I can't tell you how rare a feat that is. What strength, drive, and sheer will it took for her to accomplish her goals! Given all the obstacles that military life throws at an Army spouse, most don't have the stomach or the perseverance to overcome them. By the time they leave the Army, many feel they are too old and worn-out to tackle the task of picking up the pieces of an abandoned career. For every Kim, there are thousands of spouses who never realize their dreams.

So, why is this important? After all, the main job of the Army is to fight and win our nation's wars, not to worry about what service members' families might need or want. My point is that an organization cannot create a caring culture if its actions don't support its words. While the Army pays lip service to the importance of having all the family members in tow, its actions don't always match. To do so, the Army would have to dramatically change its model and show spouses they are truly part of the work community—that their value isn't secondary.

Perhaps this is an impossible feat for the Army to accomplish, and maybe it's not that important in the whole scheme of things. But I would suggest that, if the Army aspires to an empathetic model, its leadership should care about it. There would be a real benefit if the Army looked closely at what impact the military lifestyle has on Army families and the overall satisfaction of its service members, particularly at the lowest levels.

A September 2021 Bloomberg headline read *US Military Faces Biggest Recruiting Hurdles in 50 Years*. The Army fell short of its recruitment goals in 2022 by 15,000 soldiers, and, overall, the military is projected to fall short by at least 21,000 active-duty service personnel in 2023, with the Army the branch of most concern. Many reasons are given for this recruiting decline. One is that it is hard to compete with private companies that offer more attractive benefits in a tight labor market. Another is that a disproportionate number of potential recruits don't meet the recruiting criteria because of obesity or moral or mental-health issues.

The Modern War Institute of West Point puts forward a third reason, suggesting that the Army needs to overhaul its entire model. "This requires a pivot from an industrial-era personnel-management model, which treats people like an inventory of interchangeable parts that must be stamped with a series of 'qualifying' assignments in environments that prioritize activity over mastery." Which is to say that the Army needs to break up the bureaucratic rigidity that exists around assignments and promotions. Instead, they should consider the benefits of allowing people to remain in the same place longer and still be competitive for promotion. The Army model can't continue to be a mere matter of filling positions with warm bodies.

In other words, the Army's management model must change from one of *execution* to one of *expertise*, with a long way to go toward the model of *empathy* that many other organizations are poised to achieve. Is it possible, while acknowledging the need for a focus on expertise, that the Army might also look at how they can create Army communities that create meaningful experiences for everyone involved?

The Office of People Analytics (OPA) released the findings of its 2019 Active Duty Spouse survey. It showed that 40% of spouses did not favor their service member staying in the military, a significantly higher percentage than in the 2012–2015 survey. If the Army wants to retain its best and brightest, shouldn't some thought be given to the needs of those who have the most influence on these service members' decisions—their families? Shouldn't the Army be looking at what changes they can make so that caring about Army families becomes more than rhetoric and halfway measures?

I'm not saying that there aren't many instances in the Army today where leaders show empathy toward soldiers and their families. I routinely had opportunities to show I cared. We sent soldiers home from combat zones who were experiencing problems on the home front because it was the right thing to do, even if policy said otherwise. If possible, we tried to send soldiers home to be present at the birth of their children. We intervened on behalf of seriously ill subordinates to allow them to retire at their current rank, when policy said they hadn't been in their positions for a sufficient amount of time. In my experience, any good leader in the Army cared in these and countless other ways on behalf of those they led. But these are all individual departures from policy, not a change in policy.

Many Army leaders felt as former Chief of Staff of the Army Erik Shinseki did—and I'm paraphrasing—*The Army isn't just about people; the Army* is *people.* And I would say most people I knew truly believed this and felt they were supporting the Army community. But is saying and believing it enough for the Army to be competitive in the future when other organizations widely embrace a business model of empathy?

In hindsight, I learned that there is a distinction between showing you care by being supportive and showing you care by being empathetic. Soldiers at all levels showed pride in the ways they "supported" their wives with the things they thought were important—sending them flowers, bragging about them, and volunteering to watch the kids for a few hours. I certainly considered myself supportive of my wife while we were in the Army. And if you ask her, she would agree. I said all the right things, spoke about her proudly, and considered us a team. But it wasn't until she went back to school and began interviewing for teaching jobs, at age 61, that I truly understood her challenges. By then, it was too late. You can't make changes and improvements simply by being supportive, by showing small gestures of support.

Vulnerability means leaders must look at their individual roles in the current status quo, not retrospectively. They must understand what isn't working for those under their care by putting themselves in their place—and then, most importantly, taking some steps to improve whatever needs to change. Without institutionalizing caring leadership behavior in this way and creating new policies to support it, the Army—and other like organizations—won't be able to compete for talent in the future.

Having said that, I understand how difficult it might be to shift to an empathy paradigm for organizations like the Army. It seems too touchy-feely—a bridge too far. The idea of it, no doubt, immediately creates concern about how exposed this approach will leave the organization. And these concerns are valid. For many organizations, making monumental changes overnight just isn't feasible.

But good leaders can help shepherd this change by modeling caring behavior within their own realms of influence and looking for opportunities to incrementally move the organization forward toward an empathetic culture. During my time leading a large distribution center for Target, I found such an opportunity.

When I joined the organization, I noticed that, when we hired first-line executives, our policies meant that we almost exclusively hired people from outside, rather than promoting from within. A minimum requirement was that candidates had to have a college degree. We recruited heavily at local colleges and universities and kept our eyes and ears open for executives at rival companies who might be looking for a new opportunity. We rarely looked within our ranks in the distribution centers for potential executives, because most hourly workers lacked college degrees.

Once I became familiar with our hiring policies, it struck me that we had no dedicated program to assess and promote our hourly team members who showed potential to do more at higher levels. When I assumed the leadership of my facility in 2012, we had only one executive out of about 50 total who'd been a former team member, and he'd gotten a college degree to make himself eligible.

In my eyes, our hourly team-member workforce (which eventually grew to 1,500) contained a wealth of potential executive talent right under our noses. Here we had a pool of candidates who had shown sterling performance over many years, were a great cultural fit, were technically competent, and had demonstrated they knew how to lead, albeit informally. At that time, Target had no hourly supervisors.

I thought all we had to do to develop this talent was put a program in place that would groom them for promotion. It seemed to me that doing this would not only show team members how much we cared about them but would also save the company the time and expense of recruiting and onboarding outside candidates. The only thing standing in the way was our policy that executives must have a college degree.

My bias was based on my experience in the Army and the success we'd had, and still do, in programs that promoted enlisted soldiers to officers. For every hundred new lieutenants in the Army, roughly 55–60% come out of ROTC, 20% from the US Military Academy (West Point), 5–8% are direct commissions—such as lawyers, doctors, dentists—and 10–15% are former enlisted soldiers who come from what's called the Officer Candidate School (OCS). High-potential noncommissioned officers can apply to go to this school, be trained to lead as an officer, and be commissioned as 2nd lieutenants upon graduation. It's a fabulous program, and many of the Army's best leaders, past and present, are the product of OCS. All this made me wonder why Target couldn't do something similar. So, I set about looking into it.

I discussed my plan to create a program in my distribution center with my boss. I proposed assessing our hourly team members—especially those who had expressed an interest in executive-level leadership, college degree or not—and putting a plan in place to develop them for eventual promotion.

Immediately, I met pushback. The usual things. Promoting someone to an executive job without a college degree was against company policy. If we made an exception for one distribution center, we'd have to do it for all of them. Lowering the requirement bar would lower the quality of candidates.

However, I felt strongly enough that I refused to let the idea go. I practically badgered my boss to allow me to run a pilot program. I showed her statistics on new executive hires and the percentage who washed out due to incompetence, a lousy cultural fit, or just a stark inability to lead. At the time, we'd been experiencing a lack of qualified candidates, on top of already-existing holes in our team. So, my boss gave me tacit approval to develop a pilot program and show her what I could do to supplement our existing external hiring process with internal candidates.

My senior leadership team and I quickly put together a comprehensive assessment-and-development program and implemented it. We started by identifying team members with potential. Part of my leadership style was to spend time on every shift to get to know the workers, and it soon became clear who our candidates would be.

One of them was Cindy, a warehouse team member who'd been with Target for nine years. In her late 20s, Cindy was a top-shelf warehouse worker. Technically expert all around, she had a sterling safety record and was well-respected on her shift by other team members—she was clearly the go-to person in her department. She was an indispensable member of our team. But she didn't have a college degree. Her leaders were hesitant to move her up because her departure would leave a void in their daily operations. I told them that excuse should *never* be the reason not to offer an opportunity to an employee.

We broached the idea of her becoming an executive, and she was hesitant. She was shy and not comfortable in large groups, showing passion only for what she did one-on-one. She lacked confidence. We asked her to give us a chance to work with her; we told her she had nothing to lose. We would give her increasingly important responsibilities so she could gain the experience she needed to excel as an executive. If, at any point, she wanted out or it didn't seem to be a good fit, she would be able to go back to her old job. She agreed.

It took about a year until she was officially promoted. Until then, we prepared her. We designed a plan that put her in situations where she could learn and demonstrate her leadership ability. These included implementing a best-practice process in her department across all shifts, analyzing a problem and proposing its solution, briefly leading a team on a specific project, and presenting a program to visiting high-level executives. All along the way, we coached her. Her confidence in front of others grew steadily with each opportunity presented to her, until we all agreed she was ready.

We promoted her to executive in early 2017, and she quickly stood out as a terrific leader. Two years later, she was promoted to senior operations manager. And Cindy was only one of many. The pilot was a resounding success.

We had designed the program well. We actively sought out people who showed potential; we didn't necessarily wait for them to come to us. We put their personal growth above our day-to-day operational needs. We crafted each developmental plan for the individual to help them in the areas they needed most and then coached them throughout the process.

When I left the company, five years after we'd begun the program, there were 15 former team members in our executive ranks, roughly a third of our total executive team. We were the most productive facility of its kind in all of Target for two years running—my last two full years with the company. Our efforts had more than paid off.

But the most important success factor in my mind—far beyond mere productivity numbers, reduced safety incidents, or any other business metrics—was the impact on our team-member morale. After implementing the program, morale soared. We had the highest Best Team Survey rankings for engagement among our workforce ever—among the highest in Target. You could literally feel a tangible excitement and positive vibe coming from our team members, both those who aspired to be promoted and those who were content with remaining in their jobs.

With this program, we showed our team we cared about them and their growth. We did more than just talk. We demonstrated our commitment by allocating resources and making a concrete investment in them as individuals. We removed an arbitrary barrier—a college degree—to help them achieve their personal and professional goals.

When I retired from Target in 2019, no other facility in the company could match the number of former team members we had in our executive ranks—not even close. My former Human Resources partner, who has gone on to positions of increased responsibility at Target, recently told me our program is not only thriving but has spread to many other facilities. On top of that, new shift-leader positions for hourly team members have been created and put in place across the organization. As I recognized long ago, these new positions address the span-of-control challenges Target had (in some departments, the ratio was one leader to sixty workers). But more critically, the positions now serve as a proving ground and steppingstone for aspiring leaders who want to lead at the executive level but lack experience.

Of everything I accomplished at Target, I am most proud of this. I was able not only to create an inclusive work community in our distribution center that gave our team a meaningful work experience but also to establish a new way of looking at work in Target's distribution centers in general.

So, I would encourage any of you who aspire to become a caring leader not only to allow yourself to be vulnerable so that you can lead with empathy but also to look around your organization. Find one policy that no longer makes sense—a policy that is a barrier to the goals, well-being, or job satisfaction of your employees. Like Target's policy that executive positions required a college degree. Like the Army's policy to report spouses' speeding tickets to the service member's commanding officer. It doesn't have to be a big thing.

Then do what it takes to change the policy. You will be surprised what removing even small obstacles can do—how much more engaged and loyal your team will become.

That's what caring leadership looks like.

You may not change your organization overnight into one that models empathy, but you will have made a start. Caring is contagious. Others will want what your team has. And you'll be responsible for helping your organization take one step closer to the future.

‹ ‹ ◆ › ›

– 13 –

CREATING A CULTURE OF COMMUNICATION

*The art of vulnerability
is the language of
communication*

We cannot have a conversation about leadership and vulnerability without talking about communication and the role it plays in making leaders exceptional. As author and presidential speechwriter James Humes once said, "The art of communication is the language of leadership." In other words, to excel as a leader, you must be a good communicator.

How else can leaders guide others through periods of change and difficulty?

How else can leaders motivate and create common goals?

I thought we should start by defining the term "good communication." Coursera, an online learning platform, defines it as: "the process of exchanging ideas, thoughts, opinions, knowledge, and data so that the message is received and understood with clarity and purpose. When we communicate effectively, both the sender and the receiver feel satisfied."

This definition highlights an important aspect of communication that some leaders miss—it is a two-way proposition. Simply putting words out into the universe isn't enough. One must be responsible for making sure the intent and meaning of those words are understood. This means leaders must also know how to fully listen to another person, to truly hear what is being said. Unfortunately, not all leaders are adept at making sure their interchanges accomplish this.

The crux of the matter, as author and playwright George Bernard Shaw said so succinctly, is that "The single biggest problem in communication is the illusion that it has taken place."

We all know that communication fails when people on the giving or receiving end:

- ▸ Don't listen to each other or to what is being said

- ▸ Are vague or unclear about what they want to say

- ▸ Don't trust or respect each other

- ▸ Have a biased agenda that precludes open and honest dialogue

- ▸ Fail to take into consideration non-verbal cues

- ▸ Talk at cross-purposes

Just knowing these are the reasons doesn't necessarily solve discourse problems, however. The very nature of communication makes mastering it difficult. No two humans view the world in the same way, and they bring these differing viewpoints into any conversation. They also bring different expectations to the table. And this can make it hard for people to be objective about what and how they share.

On top of that, according to Princeton University, everyone expresses themselves in one of four different styles. Some people communicate passively and defer to others instead of expressing their opinions openly. Others are passive-aggressive and only pretend to defer, while making it abundantly clear they disapprove. Then, there are the aggressive communicators, who can be defensive and hostile as they combatively assert their own views, often steamrolling over opposing ideas. Finally, there are those who are assertive communicators—open and honest with their expressions and respectful of others while making their opinions known.

In any given situation, conversation, or discussion, there can be any combination of communication styles at play. Effective leaders need to understand not only their own style but those of their peers, bosses, and subordinates. They need to be able to "read" their audiences at each and every encounter, and possibly modify their approach accordingly.

Plus, communication is always more than just the words spoken. It includes the tone, mood, inflection, and intent that go along with the words. Numerous nonverbal cues can also change what is heard or interpreted. For example, if a person says, "This isn't what I expected," with a wide smile, others will likely assume the person is pleasantly surprised. The same sentence said with a frown would mean the exact opposite.

Sometimes no words at all need to be spoken, and still, these nonverbal cues speak volumes. During a meeting, a boss says,

"This is what we're going to do. No one has a problem with it, do they?" An employee opens their mouth and then quickly closes it, looks down at the paper in front of them, and taps it nervously with a pencil. No words are exchanged, but it is clear that the employee has second thoughts about voicing an objection.

While we normally don't think about it, most conversations involve not only the mouth but the eyes as well. Something as infinitesimal as pupils contracting sends a nonverbal message that the person is on guard or wary. (For this reason, for example, many professional poker players wear sunglasses at the table). How many times have you heard someone say something to the effect of, "They didn't have to say anything—I could read it in their eyes"?

This is why email and other non-face-to-face communication can pose opportunities for misunderstanding—there are no surrounding indicators to add meaning to the words or situation. The person who receives the electronic communication must interpret the message in a vacuum.

Finally, there is the context of the communication. Every organization has its own culture. The same words spoken in one culture can have an entirely different meaning when spoken in another culture. Say one organization has a culture of innovation and breaking rules, and another has a culture of control and adhering to norms and standards. The phrase "So much for regulations" would have a very different connotation depending on which place of business they were spoken. In the first case, the words condone ignoring regulations as a positive, and in the second, they would be a comment on problematic behavior.

You can see how the art of communication can become very nuanced and complicated. Simply barking out orders, expecting them to be followed, and then being surprised with the fallout when they aren't shouldn't be the playbook for good leadership. Leaders must be fully aware of all aspects of their communication and take full responsibility for what is said and its aftermath.

That requires vulnerability on more than one level.

First, leaders must be willing to honestly assess their own communication skills. They must determine which style they have and take a hard look at whether they need to modify it. Earlier in the book, I mentioned that the communication style I used in the Army didn't translate very well into an environment like Target. I had to modify my style and become less aggressive and more assertive and open. To do that, I had to be vulnerable enough to take feedback from others and use it to actively change my behavior. It's important to be cognizant as a leader that communication is always situational. Being a successful communicator in one instance does not guarantee you will be so in another. The only way to know if your message has registered with someone else is to ask for feedback, and that's always a vulnerable proposition.

Second, leaders must be fully accountable for managing the interactions within their team or working group. If there is a communication breakdown, they must take responsibility for it and take any steps necessary to correct it—even if the problem lies with another member of the team.

The leader must set an example, model appropriate communication behavior, and manage team members so that every individual understands how team members are expected to interact. Bad behavior in any team reflects on the leader—either the leader has created a culture where such behavior is acceptable, or they haven't been clear in setting behavioral expectations.

As President Harry S. Truman was fond of saying, "The buck stops here."

This is often the most difficult thing for leaders to do. There is a temptation to want to lay the blame for poor communication elsewhere, often understandably so, for example, to blame a team member for running their own agenda, blame a subordinate for taking a right turn when it should have been left, or to plead ignorance. However, being the leader means showing the way or being the person who says, "I am ultimately responsible." By accepting this accountability, leaders automatically make themselves vulnerable. They have agreed to be culpable for whatever goes wrong. And there is nothing more powerful—or scary—than taking the position "I am accountable, no matter what."

When leaders accept this full responsibility, a funny thing happens. They have skin in the game. They've put themselves on the line. They have a personal investment in the organization and the people they lead. It's the difference between renting and owning. They have no choice but to be the best communicator possible because that's the only tool available for leading in a fully accountable fashion.

And it does pay off. By taking full responsibility and not blaming others, leaders create an opening for their team members to rally around and help solve whatever problem has occurred. If leaders don't do this, but instead look to lay the blame elsewhere, teams quickly devolve into every-person-for-themselves behavior, and the problems get worse.

This can have disastrous results. In 2022, the online auction company eBay experienced one of its worst public-relations nightmares because of a supposed communication error. Two former eBay executives, James Baugh and David Harville, were sent to prison after launching a harassment campaign against the creators of an online newsletter that was critical of eBay. In August of 2019, this online newsletter released an article about a lawsuit that eBay had brought against Amazon, accusing the online retailer of poaching eBay's sellers. It was written by Ina Steiner, one of the editors, and it wasn't the first article to voice criticism of eBay. Immediately, eBay executives bristled.

The CEO at the time, Devin Wenig, quickly shot off a message to another high-level company executive that said, "If you are ever going to take her down . . . now is the time," referring to Ina Steiner. That executive forwarded Wenig's message to Baugh and added his own spin on the situation, calling Steiner a troll who needed to be "burned down."

What ensued was an extensive harassment campaign against Ina and her husband, led by Baugh and Harville. The Steiners received intimidating and often threatening Twitter messages. Anonymous packages arrived at the couple's home, including a box of live spiders, cockroaches, a funeral wreath, and a book about surviving the loss of a spouse. Dozens of bizarre emails filled Ina Steiner's inbox from unlikely places, like an irritable bowel syndrome support group and the Communist Party of the United States.

Criminal charges were brought against Baugh and Harville, who both claimed only to be executing the wishes of eBay's senior leadership, which included the message Wenig had sent that started the whole fiasco. Wenig himself wasn't criminally charged in the case, although he did step down as CEO in 2019. Throughout the whole ordeal, he maintained he knew nothing about the harassment, purporting that the message to "take her down" was taken out of context. His position: through no fault of his own, his words were misinterpreted by rogue subordinates who saw a threat against eBay and devised deplorable actions on their own initiative. In no way had he expected Baugh and Harville to proceed with the strange criminal acts they did. He merely meant that legal steps should be set in motion against the Steiners.

In other words, he placed the blame for what happened squarely on others. At no point did he look at how his initial communication might have been at cause. Granted, arguably there is ambiguity in the words "take her down." But shouldn't Wenig have taken responsibility for making his intent clear in the first place? Shouldn't he have specified what outcome he was looking for and who was responsible for making it happen? And finally, shouldn't he, as the company leader, have modeled a way of behaving that would have made his executives understand that certain actions were not acceptable, no matter how vague his communication? The fellow executive who suggested Ina Steiner should be "burned down" obviously took a page from Wenig's book.

The leaders at the highest levels of eBay showed a severe lack of communication skills at best and no accountability at worst. But major snafus like this don't happen out of the blue. They almost always happen in companies with a poor communication culture—one that encourages negative and careless communication. And that always starts at the top.

Although not to the same degree, I saw similar communication mistakes made frequently while coaching senior Army leaders on the military decision-making and planning process. Army leaders must be able to deliver their intent and guidance for an upcoming operation to their staff in such a manner that everyone knows what must happen and who is responsible for what. If they do this badly, the likelihood of the operation failing increases. It's like dominoes. Poor communication gets repeated down the line, open to misinterpretation at each step, and before you know it, the whole process has collapsed under the weight of misunderstandings.

Time and time again, I'd see a colonel's guidance poorly stated, vague, too specific in areas that didn't matter, or scattershot. Based on this direction, the resulting plans that came back left a lot to be desired. Invariably, these colonels were frustrated. They complained the plan wasn't what they'd envisioned and sent the team back to the drawing board. But having a vision or idea isn't enough. It must be articulated so that others can see the same thing. If not, the most elegant and brilliant ideas are lost. Plus, there is a cost. Even if the guidance was clearer the second time around, you can imagine the whole team's frustration at how much efficiency, time, and money was wasted in redoing the plan.

This is why Humes considers the art of communication so important for leaders. Just because we share a common language and can talk with others doesn't mean we can communicate effectively. To do so takes a lot of work and commitment.

First, leaders must task themselves with responsibility for the entire communication process on any given project or task—and not only for *delivering* it but for making sure those who receive it understand it satisfactorily all the way down the line. Leaders must internalize Truman's "The buck stops here." Then, they must do their homework so they are aware of all the key areas that need to be part of the conversation so that all moving pieces are covered—the potential roadblocks, past history, and necessary resources and expertise. Ignorance is never an excuse. They must assess and understand the people on their team, understand how they express themselves, and learn how best to collaborate with them.

Leaders must then craft their messages in a way that eliminates as much ambiguity, vagueness, confusion, and misinterpretation as possible. Finally, good leaders must be open to feedback all along the way, so that if any communication missteps do occur, they can be corrected before they blow up into major issues. Like what happened at eBay.

Communicating this rigorously is a tall order. Especially because communication is situational—every instance is different and can't be handled in a cookie-cutter manner. This is especially true in the age of around-the-clock emails, text messages, and tweets that have become the most common means of interacting between leaders and subordinates, especially in our post-Covid world of remote and hybrid work environments.

In recent years, we've seen a drop in the number of work meetings where we converse face-to-face with each other. That means we've lost many of the nonverbal aspects of communication we normally rely on, such as body language, gestures, changes in breathing, and involuntary reactions such as blushing. This includes Zoom and similar internet forums used for remote communication that can't be considered true "in-person" interactions. Too much of what goes on in these forums isn't observed. With more than a dozen people on a call, each becomes a small headshot on the screen. It's difficult to see everyone at once or pick up body language that is off-camera. Conversation can become awkward because many of the nonverbal cues that we normally use to guide discussions are missing. Given this, leaders must understand whatever dynamic is going on in each specific interaction and find ways to mitigate the challenges that come with those dynamics.

I realized how important clarity and precision were in my written communication at Target. Once, I was particularly direct with someone at headquarters in an email, and my comments were taken the wrong way. As a result, I modified my usual approach to writing and sending emails. I started running some of my emails by trusted individuals for their feedback. Sometimes, I asked my executive assistant or HR manager. Or, if it was a communication to higher-ups that included respectful pushback, I occasionally ran it by a subordinate as a developmental opportunity for them. Another set of eyes and a reaction from a third party proved invaluable in ensuring my comments weren't offensive, too direct, open to other interpretations, vague, or overstated.

Often in the Army, I did a similar thing when I wanted objective feedback about my message. I always work best if I can think out loud, depending on the audience. So, I would bring a principal subordinate or two into a room and go over my thoughts about how to communicate an upcoming guidance. My subordinates would act as sounding boards and give me ideas and input to make my message stronger. They would provide feedback on how my words landed with them and give me insight into how well I was communicating my intent. By making myself vulnerable in this way, I created an environment where input was welcome, ideas sought after, and out-of-the-box thinking encouraged. After going through this process, when I did deliver my final guidance, I was confident that the communication was satisfactorily doing its job.

What I've come to realize over the years is that just the act of communicating makes a person vulnerable. Every time you put an expression of yourself out into the world, it is assessed. Once an email is launched, once the words come out of your mouth, or once that tweet is transmitted, there's no going back. Your words and thoughts are in the stratosphere. Forever. Context is lost. Forever. Backpedaling, further clarification, or apologies after the fact are always less effective than getting the message right at the start. Saying "I didn't mean that" is often lost in the wind. Whatever impression you've made remains smoldering out there like an ember that never dies.

I found both in the Army and at Target that making yourself vulnerable *beforehand*—asking for feedback from trusted colleagues—almost always ensures that your communication will be spot on, and it will save you from embarrassment or worse. Proactive vulnerability or putting yourself at risk with a small number of trusted people is always preferable to exposing yourself to thousands of strangers.

Some people think that running every piece of correspondence past someone else is time-consuming and unnecessary. I'm not advocating that. What I'm proposing is for leaders to understand their communication strengths and weaknesses, and understand the kind of communication that is sensitive, important, and potentially controversial. And then for the same leaders to develop a plan and take the necessary steps to make sure they are rigorous about making their expression as effective as it can be, before actually delivering it.

At some point, every leader will be tasked with leading others through difficult times or transformational change, both of which cause a lot of anxiety, concern, and fear in people. How things are conveyed during these times matters. Being a good communicator really counts, and leaders should lean on others to help them. If communication during a crisis or major change isn't open, honest, informative, specific, and empathetic, leaders will have a hard time getting people to rally around them. Although I haven't researched it, I suspect most failed attempts to enact significant change can be traced back to poor communication.

When I was at Target, I was asked to lead my facility through a transformational change. Beginning in 2015, we started an almost 18-month process to turn our regional distribution center (RDC), supporting about 70 stores in 5 Midwestern states, into an upstream distribution center (UDC), supporting approximately 700 stores in 19 states. It meant roughly tripling our 500-member workforce to almost 1,500, automating large portions of our processes, and changing the types of products we handled. We were part of a $250 million endeavor and one of three RDCs being transitioned.

This was major change. Before this, our facility handled all the products found in the Target stores in our states. In other words, we warehoused and distributed a large number of distinct items, but in limited quantities. If unexpected demand for an item happened, our stock could be depleted quickly, and we'd have to look outside our distribution area to find more. This sometimes made it difficult to get products to customers in the time frame they wanted.

Under the new model, our center would become the "upstream" part of the supply chain—a distribution center designed to be more responsive to these unexpected demands for certain products. Instead of handling the full range of Target products, we would be focusing mainly on those items whose demand was hard to predict, for example, brand-new products, seasonal items, fashion apparel, or accessories. The idea was that by moving larger quantities of these unpredictable items into upstream distribution centers like ours, the supply chain would be more agile in responding to unforecast or situational demands.

As you can imagine, this major shift in our center's purpose, processes, and scope worried some of the employees who worked there. They suspected we might not have their best interests at heart. Automating parts of our distribution process meant some jobs would no longer exist. They wondered how we would incorporate two to three times as many people in our facility. They were concerned that our relationships with the stores we served would change—and there were many other anxieties.

I had done my share of leading change before I came to Target. Sometimes in the Army, we had to introduce newly fielded equipment and replace existing models. Once, as a brigade commander, I had to implement changing the soldiers' headgear. The Army was replacing ball caps with berets—a simple enough change, but one that carried strong feelings about the traditional uniform. I learned very quickly that it is not only the logistics that matter when implementing any kind of major change but also the emotions and concerns that come with it.

Given this background, I knew that a key component to successfully leading my distribution center through this change was to have an effective communication strategy. The first thing I did was familiarize myself with all the issues my team had going into the project. Then I made a commitment to be the face of the change we were undergoing—the main person my team could freely talk to about it and offer their ideas and concerns in a safe space.

Here's what my communication strategy entailed:

1. I held regular planning meetings with my direct reports to discuss the transition, talk about how to convey what was going on, and get feedback. It was also a good opportunity to make sure my leadership team was on the same page.

2. In those meetings, we developed consistent messaging about the transition, based on the major concerns we knew were utmost on the team's minds, such as continually reiterating, *Yes, we are automating, but we are also creating jobs. If you have a skill that is being phased out, we'll train you on a new task. We want to retain all of you.* And, *Be proud—we've been chosen to be part of a major change to improve Target's supply chain and service to our guests.* Our goal was to provide the most accurate, up-to-date information, allay our team's worries, show how our center fit into the big picture of Target's retail logistics strategy, and develop pride and interest in being part of it.

3. We set up standard monthly meetings for the entire team. I personally put together the presentations and had my direct reports participate, so everyone could see we were united. We opened the meetings up at the end for questions that we answered honestly, based on the information we had.

4. We also posted answers to questions on message boards around the facilities.

5. We carried this same messaging in ongoing department meetings, one-on-ones, and informal meetings.

6. We followed up the messaging with our actions. For example, for those whose skills were no longer needed, training programs and paths to new jobs were, indeed, delivered.

7. If new information changed, and what had been said previously was no longer accurate, we shared with the team honestly why circumstances had changed and how it would affect them. The idea was not to have any surprises.

In one of the early planning meetings with my direct reports about the team-wide monthly meetings, a direct report asked me, "What if someone asks us a question we don't have the answer to?"

"We'll tell them we don't know," I said.

Another direct report frowned. "Is that wise? Won't they think we're hiding something?"

"Or worse," the first one added. "They might think we don't know any more than they do."

It struck me that this is one of the fears that causes leaders to make mistakes when communicating. They think that, if they don't have all the answers, people won't follow them.

"Some might," I nodded. "But we're telling the truth. If we try to sidestep it, gloss it over, or make something up, they'll soon figure out that we're not being entirely honest or open about what's happening. They won't trust us. Our team is smart. They understand this is a major, 18-month process with a lot of moving parts."

We spent the next few minutes talking about the implications of saying, "I don't know." We examined how saying it could be a positive thing if done right. Just saying, "I don't know," without following up, sends a signal that the leader doesn't think the question is important, even if the words by themselves are honest. But when a leader admits they don't know, promises to follow up, and gets back to the person, it creates a real opportunity. It takes the communication from a one-dimensional to a two-dimensional level. The words themselves are honest, and the follow-up demonstrates the leader meant them and cared. And what better way is there to show that leadership can be trusted and is worth following than showing it cares? My direct reports agreed this was the best approach for us to take, and it became part of the communication strategy.

Although, as with all transformational change, there were bumps along the way, our center came out the other side not only a much-improved link in Target's retail logistics chain but a much more cohesive leadership group with a motivated team. This is what good communication can do. This is what it means to develop a culture of communication within your sphere of influence.

The last point I'll make has to do with taking responsibility. I think we can all agree that thinking before speaking is a wise choice. But even the best leaders occasionally say something they regret. We are all human, after all. What separates good leaders from bad is how they handle their misstatements.

In recent years, we've seen a trend toward an unwillingness to admit mistakes, verbal or otherwise. The eBay executives are just one example. There is a tendency to deny, cast blame on others, or double down rather than admit the truth. While this appears to have proven beneficial enough that a whole swath of politicians and celebrities have adopted it as a strategy, it does not make them good leaders, and I believe time will prove this. They certainly won't be studied as examples or models of good leadership.

Take Dan Quayle, who was vice president from 1989 to 1993. He was widely known to misspeak, sometimes alarmingly. After a series of public statements that were incorrect, inappropriate, or just confounding, reporter Sam Donaldson asked him to comment on them. Quayle's response was, "I stand by all the misstatements that I've made"—a kind of admitting to not admitting. His response certainly didn't make Dan Quayle a trustworthy person who people were eager to follow. He came across as doubling down on vacuity. No one remembers much else about Dan Quayle. Rather than being remembered as a leader to be emulated, he goes down in the history books as a joke. This is the true result of not being willing to take responsibility for what you say.

When good leaders make a misstatement, they should admit it and correct it. When what they say causes discomfort or pain to someone else, they should immediately make a sincere apology and then take whatever action is necessary to repair the hurt the words caused. A sincere apology is one in which the speaker takes full responsibility for what was said, explains the circumstances that led to the comment, shows remorse, and then demonstrates it will not be repeated. Like much about good communication, this requires a leader to be vulnerable.

When I'd been at Target for about a year, I knew enough about the company's culture to be dangerous. Every quarter, my senior team and I would conduct what we called "Talent Day." We'd meet and discuss our executives in terms of their potential, developmental needs, and areas for performance improvement. In discussing John, a particular operations manager, who'd been in his job for about three years, I was blunt about my opinion. In the limited interactions I'd had with him, he'd done little to impress me—he'd been less than engaging and seemed to go out of his way to avoid me. He worked the evening shift Saturday through Monday, a shift that was particularly hard to staff, and I hadn't spent as much time with him as with other operations managers. During our discussion, I told my senior team not only was I unimpressed with John, but I questioned how he'd even become an operations manager in the first place. I saw my senior team exchange looks with the woman who was his manager, but didn't think much of it.

She came to see me later that day. "Your comment just wasn't fair, Mike," she said. "I want you to know that John has made significant progress as an operations manager since he started." She proceeded to fill me in on all the ways he had done so.

As I listened, I realized that my comments had not only been made without full knowledge of the situation, but it was clear that I had insulted her, too. By saying I couldn't understand how he'd become an operations manager, I'd criticized her hiring and management ability.

"Do you realize how hard it is to find good people for that shift?" she added. "John really likes to work those hours. And how can you and the rest of the senior team accurately assess John's performance when you hardly ever spend time on that shift? You're not giving him the same opportunities or access you give his peers."

She warned that it wasn't a good idea to write off marginal execs on that shift without understanding the big picture.

What she said made me look at John in a whole new way and reminded me that the purpose of Talent Day wasn't to publicly express my biased perceptions of our staff, but to collectively agree on how to develop our staff. I could clearly see that my words had, in fact, been unfair and unnecessarily critical—something the leader of a team shouldn't do.

At the earliest opportunity the next day, I apologized to the entire senior team for my comments. I explained that I spoke without knowing all the facts or circumstances and that I had been unfair not only to John but also to his boss and the senior team. As their leader, speaking so cavalierly about an employee and his managers was simply not acceptable. I pledged not to use Talent Day as a forum for my limited perceptions and also suggested we find a way to have the senior team spend more time on that particular shift.

That led us to put together a schedule so that members of the senior team would regularly come in on Saturday through Monday evenings. We put in place a specific engagement plan for those evenings to allow us to get to know the executives on that shift better, understand their developmental needs, and make them feel they were being treated in the same way as the other executives on our team.

When miscommunication is handled like this, it does a number of things. Instead of asking everyone to pretend nothing has happened, it puts an end to the incident and means that the upset won't resurface at a later date. It addresses whatever needs to be changed to prevent the same thing from happening again. In my case, it was not only my pledge to change my behavior but also the implementation of a new schedule for senior leaders.

If all these things happen, you will know your apology is sincere—everyone will be left feeling satisfied. When miscommunication is handled properly, it creates an opening, not a shutting down among team members.

I hope you see that leaders cannot be effective without mastering communication. Communication is the sole currency of human interaction, and little can be accomplished without it. Relationships would be nonexistent. Knowing all of the nuances of communication, the way people express themselves, and the group dynamics of conversation are only a part of what a leader must do. Leaders must develop a culture of communication within their teams that allows for optimal two-way discourse. Finally, leaders must be 100 percent responsible for making communication work, and they can do that only by being willing to show their vulnerability.

I believe that the art of vulnerability is the language of communication.

‹ ‹ ◆ › ›

$-14-$

NAVIGATING THE PITFALLS OF BEING VULNERABLE

There's no faking vulnerability

Vulnerability is in vogue. Google the topic, and you will find a growing number of blogs, websites, and experts extolling its virtues. Many consultants and leadership coaches have embraced the idea that vulnerability improves effectiveness and are incorporating it into their advice. There are even training and certification programs, such as "The Daring Way," based on Brené Brown's book *Daring Greatly*. Organizations like Target are continually searching for ways to include the concept in their management and human-resource programs. Vulnerability is fast becoming an asset, not a liability.

But, as with many intangible things, being vulnerable is not something that can be easily taught. It isn't a tangible skill that can be learned by following steps, like how to download an app or build a chicken coop. Vulnerability can't be turned on or off at will, trotted out for appearances' sake, or faked. It must be a genuine expression of the self. And there is always the risk that making yourself vulnerable will backfire.

Let's examine again the kind of vulnerability that makes leaders effective. First, it must be an authentic expression of oneself. Faking it until you make it doesn't work (unless you are an A-list actor or a sociopath). Second, it must be unrehearsed and relative to the moment. Vulnerability can't be a non-sequitur that comes from left field or something cut and pasted for every occasion. Third, there can't be an underlying agenda or end goal in mind—no quid pro quo or desire to manipulate the situation or person. True vulnerability should inspire trust, bring down barriers, and appeal to everyone's basic humanity. It should be a genuine moment of connection.

In August 2009, after my Iraq deployment, I took command of Fort Knox in Kentucky. A month later, I officiated a ceremony to commemorate first responders on the anniversary of 9/11. It was a beautiful September day, still warm but with a chill in the morning air. Folding chairs had been set up on the parade field under a canopy adjacent to a reception tent supplied with coffee, water, Danish, and fruit. I was the first speaker, followed by the chief of the Fort Knox Fire Department, who would then ring an old-fashioned fire bell (a mini-looking Liberty Bell) and ask for a moment of silence for the fallen.

I started my remarks by saying, "I heard an incredible story this morning that I want to share with you." The Fort Knox High School football team had played an away game at a nearby high school in a district that couldn't afford its own school band. At the time, the Fort Knox football team was the worst in the region. They hadn't won a game in a long time (maybe in years) and were a running joke in the area. Keep in mind that students at Fort Knox were always coming and going because of military moves, so the team was perpetually at a disadvantage.

The game was about to start. But because the home team didn't have a band or audio equipment to play music, the playing of the national anthem had to be skipped. At the moment when it was usually played, to the surprise of the spectators, the Fort Knox football players linked arms. They walked out onto the field. Every player belted out, *"O, say can you see,"* finishing up with a resounding, *"O'er the land of the free and the home of the brave,"* without musical accompaniment.

At this point in my remarks, I had to pause. I was moved to my core thinking about these young players—who were likely to lose their game—showing such generosity and spirit. They had selflessly given an *a cappella* gift to their opponents, the spectators in the stands, first responders, and their country. Unexpected emotion welled up, and my eyes filled. I struggled to continue, and a couple of times I had to stop and compose myself. I could see everyone looking from me to my wife, perhaps wondering what the deal was with the new commander. The fire chief seemed ready to jump in and save me. At that point, I simply apologized for my emotion, explaining why these kids had so moved me, why their behavior was indicative of the selflessness the first responders had exhibited on 9/11, and how they reminded me of those I'd recently served with in Iraq—some who'd given life and limb.

There is no more vulnerable feeling than standing in front of a group of people, tears in your eyes, throat constricted. But no one in the stands that day thought any less of me. In fact, my willingness to open up helped me establish myself in my new command and connect with people on a level that might otherwise not have happened as quickly. I hadn't planned it. My emotion surprised me as much as it did them. But my vulnerability worked for me that day because it was a genuine expression of what I felt, completely relevant to the event, and I didn't expect to receive anything in exchange.

However, that's not the way it always goes. At some point in our lives, everyone experiences the squirming urge to escape from someone who shares something too personal and the awkwardness of not knowing how to respond. Or perhaps we find ourselves on the other side of the equation and, having overshared, are distanced by others. In these moments, there is obviously vulnerability being exhibited—we're putting ourselves all out, after all. On the surface, these moments are no different from mine at Fort Knox.

However, three very important things are at work in these instances that make a huge difference. Context, level of trust, and motivation. And they matter. Sharing something of a personal nature out of context with the situation or conversation is the surest way to shut down an interaction. In the same way, if trust hasn't been established, the odds of things backfiring go up exponentially. And if one is sharing for the express purpose of gaining something—sympathy, domination, forgiveness, acceptance—it will be ill-received. As Brené Brown says in her book *Daring Greatly*, "Using vulnerability is not the same as being vulnerable; it's the opposite—it's armor."

Let's examine these three things in more detail.

Sharing personal, vulnerable things with others out of context is much like inappropriately airing political or religious beliefs in the wrong setting. Especially the workplace. The end results are the same. It alienates others and contributes nothing.

In the early fall of 2007, I was the deputy commanding general of the 4th Infantry Division at Fort Carson, Colorado. I presided over the funeral of a soldier who was killed in Iraq. Army policy at the time was that funerals for soldiers killed in combat were presided over by a general officer to honor the soldier's sacrifice and ensure perfection of their funeral service. I presided over 10 of them while stateside before and after my own deployments.

This task was always a top priority for general officers. It involved contacting the soldier's combat unit and finding out about the soldier—how they died, what they were like, and other personal details. I would also contact the soldier's family. Then I'd meet with them at the viewing the day before the funeral to explain how the ceremony would go and determine who would receive the flag presented by me on behalf of a grateful nation. Often, I'd also meet with the family one-on-one to ensure they were receiving whatever assistance they needed from the Army Office of Casualty Affairs. Finally, at the funeral, I would eulogize the soldier, escort the spouse or parent, and make sure everything went smoothly. It was a sobering duty but a fitting way to honor the sacrifice of the fallen.

The point is that everything about the ceremony was supposed to be about the soldier and his family. My job was to make sure no other agenda marred the occasion.

On this particular day, the funeral was in Cheyenne, Wyoming. With my aide and driver, we left Fort Carson the day before to attend the viewing that evening. My aide, Roger, a first lieutenant, had been with me for about four months. Just the week before our trip, I walked by his desk and noticed a stack of flyers and brochures for the then-presidential candidate Ron Paul stacked on it.

Pointing at his desk, I asked, "Roger, what's all this about?"

A tall, fairly introverted man, Roger looked at the campaign paraphernalia and explained a bit sheepishly that he was a volunteer for Ron Paul's campaign.

Without being too severe, I said, "You understand you're free to do whatever you want out of uniform and on your own time. But the Army is very clear that, while in uniform, as a representative of the U.S. Army, you're expected not to espouse or display your specific political biases. That material needs to be out of sight here at work."

It's important to understand that the Army prides itself on being an apolitical organization. Like most officers, during my entire career, I registered to vote with the No Party Affiliation designation to avoid aligning myself with a particular party. How I voted had no place at work. While this is explicitly understood in the Army, it's generally a good rule for any business or organization to avoid the sharing of political or religious views in the workplace—especially when the work at hand has nothing to do with them.

Roger nodded, gathered up the brochures, and put them away. I thought that was the end of it.

So, you can imagine my consternation in Cheyenne when I left my hotel room the morning after the viewing and strode to our car. I stopped. I hadn't seen the back of the car the day before. There, in the bright morning light were two magnetic Ron Paul bumper stickers on the back of the government sedan. Without my knowing it, while clearly dressed in Army uniforms, we'd traveled in broad daylight from Colorado to Cheyenne broadcasting my aide's political beliefs. No one could miss the government license plates.

With these bumper stickers in full view, we'd attended a viewing to honor a fallen soldier whose family's political beliefs could have been entirely different from my aide's. We'd driven for two hours on Interstate 25 and around Cheyenne showing support for a political candidate—something that just isn't done in the Army. It was not only inappropriate and disrespectful for such a solemn occasion but also defied Army standards.

"What the hell, Roger?" I frowned, standing behind the car, hands on my hips.

Roger hung his head. "Sorry, sir."

"You're damned right you're sorry."

"I slipped them on before we left. Just a couple of bumper stickers," he almost pleaded. "I didn't think it would do any harm."

I lit into him, reminding him of our previous discussion. "Get rid of them," I said.

He knelt and quickly removed them.

"This isn't over," I added. "We've got a funeral to attend."

We drove in silence to the church and completed our task.

On the surface, a couple of bumper stickers don't seem like a major offense. But the context of the situation made them blatantly out of place. The fact that my aide had thoughtlessly put them on the car of a general officer presiding over a funeral that was intended to be a show of respect and gratitude for a fallen soldier's family made them cringeworthy—like the worst kind of *oversharing*. Clearly, my aide's motivation for putting the stickers on the car had nothing to do with honoring the soldier and his family. It had to do with his own desire to broadcast his political choices to the outside world, to show his personal support and enthusiasm for his presidential pick. It was a selfish act.

That afternoon on the two-hour ride back to Fort Carson, with my driver wishing he could be anywhere but in the car, I told Roger in no uncertain terms that he'd embarrassed me as well as the Army. I let him know I was seriously considering relieving him from duty and sending him back to the unit he'd come from before becoming my aide. I ended up not doing so—we were just weeks away from deploying for 15 months, and training a new aide was impractical. But when I later gave him his officer-efficiency report, I rated him subpar largely because of this issue, which showed a clear lack of judgment.

Target Corporation also did not allow employees to display their political affiliation. When one of my team members wore a Donald Trump T-shirt to work, I instructed his immediate supervisor to have him take it off or cover it up. Its mere presence upset some of the other team members who were Hispanic and unhappy about Trump's comments about Mexicans, calling them "rapists" and "murderers."

This illustrates why sharing certain things in the workplace out of context is not a good idea. And this proves true no matter how vulnerable the thing shared makes a person. It can have unexpected consequences and even be career-limiting. It can also cause distress to others within the organization. Sharing personal information at the wrong place and time is a self-serving act, no matter how vulnerable you may be. Context does matter.

Oversharing can also be strategically manipulative and cause mistrust. A friend of mine who was a vice president for a Fortune 500 company went on a business trip with her boss. She'd been working with him for only a few months. After their business concluded, they agreed to meet in the hotel lobby the next morning to catch a taxi to the airport.

He showed up, hair still wet from a shower, a paper cup of coffee in his hand. They stood by the revolving door, waiting for the cab. He sighed, ran a tired hand over his face, and took a sip of his coffee.

Making small talk, she asked, "Did you sleep well?"

He paused a moment and then turned and gave her a sly grin. "I got me a spanking."

She didn't know what to say. She clutched the handle of her roller bag and looked away. Finally, she managed, "How nice for you," before excusing herself to get her own cup of coffee. A third member of their party showed up, and they headed for the airport with nothing more said about the subject.

If she'd been a long-time peer and male, perhaps his sharing would have been less awkward. But she wasn't. She hadn't worked for him long enough for any significant trust to be built between them. And she was a female subordinate.

All the way to the airport in the cab, she wondered why he'd felt compelled to say what he did. Prior to the trip, he'd mentioned in a staff meeting, "What goes on the road, stays on the road." Maybe he was testing her? Maybe he thought he was being funny? Maybe it was his way of keeping her at a distance? A way to keep her in her place, dominate her? She was the only woman who reported to him, and she often felt excluded. Or maybe he just wanted to project a certain macho image. What she did know for certain was his comment wasn't a genuine, heartfelt bit of sharing. He had another agenda behind his words even if she wasn't sure exactly what it was. The interaction did little to create a connection between the two. It simply put her on guard and made her wary.

Usually, people can tell when there is an agenda behind something being shared. In the 1960s, Robert McNamara was

U.S. Secretary of Defense and the principal architect of the U.S. involvement in the Vietnam War. John F. Kennedy had appointed McNamara as Secretary of Defense in 1961, impressed with his intellect. McNamara had earned a reputation as an analytical genius with Ford Motor Company. As Secretary of Defense, he turned around the management of the Department of Defense and brought a systems-analysis approach to running it.

At the same time, he presided over a massive escalation of troops in Vietnam. As the number of troops increased, so did the casualties, and public support for the war began to erode. By the fall of 1964, the war in Vietnam had become an all-consuming obsession of McNamara. By the time he left office in 1968, half a million American soldiers had been sent to Vietnam, with more than 36,000 deaths and nearly 100,000 wounded. When the war finally ended in 1975, those numbers were 58,000 and 150,000, respectively.

While McNamara was Secretary of Defense, he knew the war was a lost cause, but he didn't share that insight with the public until 27 years after leaving the Pentagon. In 1995, he wrote the book *In Retrospect: The Tragedy and Lessons of Vietnam*, in which he denounced the war and said it had been futile. His book drew mostly scorn, vilification, and rage when it was published. In the words of *Washington Post* author David von Crehle in an April 24, 1995 review of the book, "Those who hated the war in Vietnam want to know why McNamara was silent when it counted. Those who supported the war say McNamara was timid then and craven now. Those who fought the war ask, 'What kind of man recommends troops for a battle he doesn't believe they can win?' And they resent McNamara for calling their struggle 'a mistake.'"

Clearly, from the response to his book, the sincerity of his confession was called into question and ulterior motives assigned. Why was he, after so many years, sharing his true thoughts? To make himself feel better? To assuage a guilty conscience so that he could look at himself in the mirror and not be ashamed? Obviously, he was not concerned with what the many families who'd lost loved ones in the war would feel upon hearing that their sacrifice had been in vain. As John Kerry, a Vietnam combat veteran, future senator, and future presidential nominee, put it during a 1971 Congressional inquiry, "How do you ask a man to be the last man to die for a mistake?"

Even if McNamara's rationale was to warn of U.S. involvement in similar wars in the future, McNamara's soul-baring method of doing so backfired because many people questioned his intent.

You can see from these three examples that sharing personal things may make a person vulnerable, but instead of creating a deeper connection and understanding, it can produce the opposite result. When, what, where, why, and with whom something is shared matters a great deal, and, if leaders are to be successfully vulnerable, they need to understand these parameters.

There is a fourth thing to consider when sharing personal things with others. Everyone has different comfort levels and personal boundaries. Some people's natural way of being is to express everything they think or feel. Others are reserved and tight-lipped, with the majority of people falling somewhere along that continuum. Given these varying approaches, we can't expect everyone to express vulnerability in the same way or at the same time. Expecting people to be vulnerable at the drop of a hat serves only to discourage authentic expression. Instead, it encourages what I call "ersatz vulnerability"—a pressure to give in to what is expected even if the heart isn't in it.

With the recent surge of interest in vulnerability within the business world, many consulting firms and experts are attempting to introduce vulnerability into their programs and offerings and make it part of business retreats, off-site trainings, and team-building events. Generally, it shows up in the form of group exercises designed to force all participants to share something personal with the group, often with a discussion afterward about how being vulnerable gave them insight or changed them.

Jordan Harbinger is a Wall Street lawyer-turned-interviewer and the creator of the podcast *The Jordan Harbinger Show*. He wrote an article focused on exactly why this sort of activity doesn't work—why it produces exactly the opposite effect of what is intended. He tells the story about a dinner he attended with entrepreneurs and artists, where the host went around the table and asked everyone to share the one thing they were most worried about at the time. The first thing that came to Jordan's mind was *I don't want to do this.* But as each person around the table spoke about their worries, he felt pressured to do the same.

"I couldn't tell you what I finally came up with," he writes. "Probably something about the company. Or the podcast. Or my frustrations about living in LA. I'm sure whatever I said had a kernel of truth to it, but I'm also pretty sure it wasn't my biggest worry at the time. In truth, my biggest worry at the time was not looking like an idiot in front of all these people. People who were brave enough to share their feelings. People who seemed way better at 'being vulnerable' than I was. People who jumped at the chance to really connect."

At the end of the evening, the host thanked everyone for "opening up," but Jordan left the dinner feeling the opposite of vulnerable, connected, and intimate. His expression of vulnerability had been forced out of him, and he felt lonelier than when he'd arrived. Years later, he realized the most vulnerable thing he could have done was decline to participate. He understood that the reason he'd felt so disconnected was that the host hadn't created true vulnerability among his guests with his exercise but rather "a scenario designed to *simulate* vulnerability."

Which is precisely what these exercises are. They are rooted in a manufactured context—not related to a real moment between people—often carried out among people with whom sufficient trust has not been built. In these scenarios, the motive of many participants is to play the game so that they gain brownie points, fit in, or are seen as team players. It is highly unlikely that the corporations and organizations putting their employees through these exercises will realize any benefits from them. Authentic vulnerability cannot be scripted, made into a process, or dictated.

Like most things of value, introducing vulnerability into an organization's culture requires creating the conditions where it can organically grow. This demands each individual leader to be willing to be authentically vulnerable and to thoroughly understand what that means. They must learn not how to *be* vulnerable but rather how *not to be afraid* of being vulnerable when the situation is right. It also means companies should hire these types of leaders, develop them, and reward them when they do show true vulnerability. If leaders don't exhibit this behavior, the rest of the organization certainly won't. And no off-site exercise can make that happen.

Authentic vulnerability can't be achieved without self-awareness. Here are some things to consider when assessing whether you are being authentically vulnerable:

Context:

1. Consider the purpose of the interaction/event/meeting, the people attending, and your role and responsibilities before you share.

2. Consider whether what you have to share belongs in the public or private sphere.

3. If you have been talking more than listening, consider stepping back and listening until you fully grasp the situation or context.

4. Given the occasion, have clear boundaries been set?

5. Is what you're sharing something that will produce a result or move the conversation forward?

Trust

1. Has sufficient trust been established with the person or group?

2. Are you aware of the hierarchy of power dynamics that are present? Trust on a peer level is not the same as trust between leader and subordinate.

3. Are you prepared for negative feedback? Rarely with large groups will you have established 100% trust, so

you will need to accept that not everyone may believe in your sincerity.

Motivation

1. Consider whether you have an agenda—what do you hope to gain from sharing?

2. Are you looking for a way to excuse your bad behavior or set up a defense?

3. Are you one-upping someone else's sharing? "If you think *that's* bad . . ."

4. Are you being empathetic and really listening or only eager to share your own experiences?

5. Has your sharing resulted in a real connection? If not, look deeper for your underlying motivation.

A final pitfall that must be addressed has to do with being vulnerable on social media. It is a unique situation, in that social media is a forum where person-to-person interaction is constrained in many ways. Something is posted, and others respond. There is no real back-and-forth conversation. There are no visual cues or nonverbal feedback. People are anonymous. The audience cannot be limited only to a trusted group. The item posted can easily be taken out of context and time, since posts remain out there long after the moment of posting has passed. Some argue that, given this reality, there is no real connection created between people through social media.

This may or may not be the case. Just know that when you post something personal on social media, you can control only one of the three areas mentioned above—your own motivation. Context and trust are taken out of your hands by the very nature of the medium. This means that there's a good chance whatever you share can and will backfire on you. I think it is especially important for leaders to understand this. Your personal life on social media is not separate from your professional life. Every day, someone makes the news because of something they posted or tweeted that can't be taken back, and sometimes the consequences are significant.

This means it's more important than ever to make sure you are posting personal things for the right reasons. You must be overly vigilant about your motivation. Leaders who "Friend" their team members on Facebook, for example, and then share something personal that has nothing to do with work may not be establishing a greater connection with their colleagues. In fact, their sharing may have the opposite effect. It might make some people feel uncomfortable and like voyeurs who have seen something they shouldn't have. Sometimes Facebook and other platforms can seem like quick vulnerability shorthand—post one thing and cover all parts of your life—but authentic vulnerability cannot be practiced in a vacuum. One size doesn't fit all.

Before posting anything, these questions should be asked: Why am I posting this? Who do I want to see it? Who will benefit from it? Am I willing to get negative comments?

A term has been bandied about social media lately— Vulnerability Porn. It's generally used to refer to posts from people who are addicted to oversharing for reasons that have little to do with honestly putting something out there they think will make others feel not so alone. Instead, these people are looking to be the next viral sensation, to fulfill an insatiable desire for validation and likes, or to monetize or commodify their trauma/pain/narrative. While it may attract many viewers drawn to the sideshow, this is "ersatz vulnerability" performed for an audience and has little to do with real connection.

Leaders cannot avoid dealing with social media in their jobs, but they don't have to use it for more sensitive personal issues or non-business-related sharing. They definitely shouldn't consider it an opportunity to show vulnerability to the world. Being vulnerable is best done in person, where everyone involved can be seen and heard.

So, as you head down your path toward becoming a more vulnerable leader, understand that, like most things worth doing, it isn't easy. There are pitfalls when authenticity is missing, and it's a mistake to think there are shortcuts or easy formulas. There is no getting around the fact that vulnerability can't be faked. Either you are, or you aren't.

‹ ‹ ◆ › ›

– 15 –

CREATING AN ENGAGED WORKFORCE

Vulnerability makes human connection blossom

Imagine going to work every day and finding the office full of people who have great enthusiasm for the work they're doing—no matter what it is. Everyone respects each other. Unasked, they jump in to help out during crunch times. They understand the purpose of their work and how it contributes to the organization's greater objectives. They feel and speak positively about their company. They care about their fellow workers, go the extra mile for customers, and are constantly looking for ways to make things better.

Does this sound like a good place to work? Do you get the idea that whoever is leading this group would be a good person to work for?

If you agree, you wouldn't be alone. This is what an engaged workforce looks like. People who feel good about the work they do are the kind of employees most companies want. According to Jon Clifton, the CEO of Gallup, "Business units with engaged workers have 23% higher profits compared with business units with miserable workers."

Study after study confirms that having engaged employees offers positive benefits to organizations. There are not only greater profits and productivity, lower absenteeism and turnover, better customer service, and safer work environments but also improved employee health and stronger recruiting. Given this, what organization wouldn't want all their employees engaged? It's a win-win. Employees are happy, and shareholders and owners are, too.

And yet, according to Gallup's latest *State of the Global Workplace: 2022 Report*, only 21% of workers worldwide are truly engaged at work. That's less than a quarter. Another 60% of global workers are emotionally disconnected on the job, and the remaining 19% are downright miserable or actively disengaged. While the numbers are a little better in the U.S. and Canada—with a 33% engagement rate instead of 21%—it still means that only a third of all workers in North America care about and are motivated by their work.

When you consider how much of a person's life is spent at work—roughly 2,000 hours a year—that's a lot of time to be feeling miserable or emotionally disconnected. Why, then, aren't more people engaged and more companies making it happen?

We've seen laudable attempts by companies in the last few decades to move this needle. Organizations have tried a whole series of incentives and perks—allowing pets at work, setting up ping-pong tables and other recreational activities, providing snacks, instituting flexible work schedules, moving to four-day work weeks, helping with day-care issues, and having monthly team lunches or other company-sponsored social events. But these changes by themselves haven't necessarily made a difference in engagement.

It seems what drives most people to be engaged at work are not always tangible things. Rather, what matters most to employees are things like being:

- ▸ recognized for their contributions

- ▸ given opportunities for growth and career development

- ▸ told the reasons why things are done the way they are

- ▸ respected and listened to

- ▸ shown their well-being matters, that they are cared about and belong

In other words, employees want to be treated like valuable human beings. When these things aren't present at work, the working environment is often full of stress, boredom, frustration, and disappointment—exactly what Gallup found when examining what lies at the heart of employee apathy and disengagement. Disengaged employees were between 46% and 83% more likely than engaged ones to report being stressed, worried, in physical pain, and angry on any given day.

These are all symptoms of burnout. When people say they are burned out, they usually mean they no longer have the emotional or physical strength to be enthusiastic or care about their work. And while even engaged people periodically experience burnout, they do so considerably less frequently. Plus, it doesn't affect their overall outlook about their jobs, because there is enough of the "good stuff" to offset whatever is causing stress.

In one of the largest studies done about burnout, Gallup found that 76% of all employees experienced burnout in their jobs—three out of four. And the top five reasons? In descending order, the major causes were: unfair treatment, unmanageable workload, unclear communication from managers, lack of manager support, and unreasonable time pressure. What all these things have in common is that, when they're present, the "good stuff" or the five things that matter most, fly out the window. In addition, these causes are also directly connected to management, or more specifically, a person's boss.

How a leader leads, then, not only makes a huge difference in whether employees are engaged—*it is the key factor.*

One of the least-engaging periods of my Army career was in 2002, when I worked in the Pentagon as the Chief of Strategy Division on the Joint Staff in the Strategy, Plans, and Policy directorate, also known as J-5. I don't think I was alone. Most active-duty people who worked at the Pentagon couldn't wait to get back into a unit in the field. The military officers who served there often talked about their most cherished view of the Pentagon (a spectacularly huge and imposing structure) being the one in their rearview mirror as they drove away for the last time.

I had just left a brigade command at Fort Riley, Kansas, and the difference between the two jobs was dramatic. At the Pentagon, there was so much work to do; everything ran at a frantic pace, and people bounced from one crisis to another. At Fort Riley, when I was on the base and not in the field training, my workday started at 8:30 a.m., after having conducted physical training at 6:30, a daily requirement. At the Pentagon, the day began typically no later than 6:30. My commute at Fort Riley had been about a mile. In DC, it was often an hour each way—I rose at

4:00 a.m. and often returned home by 7:30 or 8:00 at night. The expected work schedule was 12 to 14 hours a day. At any given moment, a million things hung over my head that easily justified staying well into the night or working through the weekend to accomplish them. Rarely was there much socializing. Everyone was just too exhausted. Talk about burnout.

I understand that part of this was the culture of the Pentagon and the time period. Twenty-five thousand people work there. The Pentagon is an incredibly complex, byzantine, labyrinthian bureaucracy, with literally thousands coming and going at any one moment. It includes all ranks and branches of the military and thousands of civilians, who are the bedrock of the institution. At the time I was there, we had invaded and were fighting a war in Afghanistan. We were developing plans to invade Iraq, which we did in March of 2003. As a nation, our strategic direction, priorities, and focus had all been turned upside down by 9/11. The Global War on Terrorism became job number one, and we were under a lot of pressure to help steer the Pentagon ship that way.

As the Army colonel assigned as Chief of Strategy Division, I had about 25 subordinates, both civilians and military officers of all branches, working for me. My immediate boss was a Navy rear admiral. His boss, the head of the J-5 directorate, was an Army lieutenant general. One of our key tasks that year was to rewrite an important document called the National Military Strategy. Based on our country's National Defense Strategy, it's part of a cascading series of documents that describe how we're going to safeguard our country, defend our way of life, secure the homeland, and protect our vital national security interests. These and other documents give guidance and establish priorities and resources so that all branches of the government are aligned when it comes to military security. Obviously, the effects of 9/11 and the shift of priorities enormously impacted this document.

Coordinating the rewrite of it with my directorate counterpart in the Office of the Secretary of Defense, as well as with other relevant government agencies, took endless back-and-forth, a very iterative process. I had to work regularly with my superior, the lieutenant general who led the J-5 directorate. Of medium height, slim, with a full head of gray hair, he was pleasant but with a serious demeanor. A bit fidgety, he had a charming smile that every so often surfaced. I found him quiet and thoughtful, with a good sense of humor on the rare occasions he used it. But mainly, he was a person busy as hell. He had a hand in nearly everything going on throughout the military at a remarkably dynamic time. Running revisions by him and getting guidance and clarification was challenging. He was under a lot of pressure and simply didn't have the time.

I'd update him about once a month. Based on moving circumstances or new guidance, he'd give me input on changes we needed to make to the document, which I expected, given all the moving pieces. But all too often, he'd send me back to revise the documents with the direction that we needed to revert to a previous iteration. I'd return to my team and tell them we had to revise all the work they'd done in the last few weeks and recreate what had been there before. It seemed as if the decision-makers were yo-yoing back and forth, with no consideration for the effect downstream. Often, I could give my team only vague reasons why this kept happening. Something like, *In the course of the last month, thinking has circled back to earlier positions.*

My subordinates would throw their hands in the air and roll their eyes.

"You're kidding, sir!"

"No way . . ." my lead writer would say, shaking his head, incredulous, even though he was a civilian who'd been in the Pentagon for 10 years and had worked on previous versions of the document.

My staff would go back to their workstations and cubicles and dive in again. I could almost see them deflate a little. There wasn't anything I could do. All I had to work with was my superior's brief, periodic guidance. I was as frustrated as they were, but I tried not to let it show.

Part of it was because I had only a transactional relationship with my superior. We hadn't really established a close, trusting relationship, in which honest, two-way feedback was possible. He knew nothing about my family, what kind of work my wife did, what my career aspirations were, or what my background was. Not that he had to—a lot was going on, and he had a dozen colonels and captains working for him. Plus, unlike at Fort Riley and other places I'd been, getting to know superiors socially wasn't an option at the Pentagon. Ceremonies were celebrated during office hours, crammed between back-to-back meetings and tasks to be accomplished. I'm not being critical of him specifically. That's how things were in the Pentagon—there simply wasn't time, especially in the aftershock of 9/11.

But when there is no personal relationship or little interest shown in a subordinate, one of the things that matters most is missing—a human connection. The subordinate can be left feeling like an interchangeable part. Like no one has their back. And in times of stress and high pressure, ironically, it's more important than ever that this "good stuff" or human connection is there to offset the demands of the work. On the converse side, bosses who don't have relationships with their subordinates can't possibly put themselves in their shoes. It gives these leaders the license not to deliver on the five things that matter most.

On top of it, my experience at my previous job, at Fort Riley, where I'd felt fully engaged, had been starkly different from my experience at the Pentagon, so I knew what I was missing. At Fort Riley, I interacted almost daily with my superiors, socialized with them, and was mentored by them. I knew about their personal lives and their families, and they knew about mine. Any long hours we worked were mitigated by this sense of belonging and being seen, of being more than just another cog in the wheel.

For this reason and others, at the end of my year in Strategy Division, I jumped at the chance to leave my position in J-5 and seek another opportunity on the Joint Staff. I applied, interviewed, and was accepted to become the Executive Assistant to the Vice Chairman of the Joint Chiefs of Staff. While the job was still at the Pentagon—I needed to work there another year—my new boss had a much different approach to his subordinates. He made it a point to mentor them, develop relationships, and show interest. Even though the environment at the Pentagon hadn't changed, my level of engagement did.

It makes sense that, when people aren't engaged in their work, they leave, hoping to find what's missing elsewhere. While there was no shortage of colonels to take my place in the J-5 Strategy Division, that's not always the case in other organizations, especially in tight labor markets or where specific expertise is required. In these situations, it's incumbent on good leaders to create an environment that encourages employees to want to stay, grow, and contribute. In other words, *to be engaged.*

To do this, leaders must understand two crucial things. First, they must determine what the most important drivers of employee engagement are for their team. Second, they must examine their own behavior and actions and notice how what they're doing detracts from or contributes to serving these drivers.

Findings in a 2021 *Harvard Business Review* study showed that leaders don't always understand what drives their employees. They found a gap between what managers think are the most important drivers and what those drivers actually are. My bosses at the Pentagon believed that we were driven by a sense of duty to our country, a desire to understand the inner workings of the defense establishment, and an aspiration for future promotion. All those things did motivate us to be at the Pentagon. We were in the military because we wanted to serve, and we were at the Pentagon to gain experience and knowledge in how the Department of Defense functioned, to give us perspective, and to broaden us professionally. But those things weren't the drivers of our day-to-day engagement.

Let's face it: People are in jobs because they need to earn money, want to get ahead, have a duty to fulfill, or want to gain knowledge. People will put up with a lot to accomplish those four things. That doesn't mean they are enthusiastic about the work, or that they give 100 percent, or that they never call in sick when they're not. It doesn't mean they're engaged. It simply means they have a goal.

Leaders need to look beyond these obvious motivations and ask themselves if employees are also receiving the five things that give employees a human connection on the job. And as I've mentioned throughout this book, one of the most assured ways to connect with others is to allow yourself to be vulnerable with them. In other words, if leaders want employees to be engaged, vulnerability is a requirement.

Good leaders must be self-aware, open to feedback, and willing to change their behavior. They need to notice the signs of employee burnout and dig deep into the causes. If they see a high rate of turnover, instead of assuming that pay levels aren't right or that they're hiring the wrong skills, they should first look at themselves. What kind of culture have they developed? What's their relationship with their subordinates? How much time do they spend listening to those who work for them? How much are they investing in their team? How well are they allowing themselves to be truly known? Leaders must continuously examine their own behavior in this area. And this examination can't be a one-time strategy; it must be a *way of being*.

Employee engagement is important because market conditions, unemployment rates, shifting skill needs, technology innovations, aging demographics, social trends, and consumer demands all impact competition for a finite pool of potential employees. Unlike the Pentagon, which had an unending supply of aspiring colonels and captains, most companies won't be able to count on factors like pay, promises of getting ahead, knowledge, and duty to keep employees on board, especially in positions that are most critical to the company's success. The future will demand managers who can build a truly engaged workforce.

Amazon Corporation is a good case study of how not to do this. When Amazon first came on the scene, it was a trailblazing company—changing the whole retail experience. Many employees were energized to be part of this innovation. It had the same cachet as start-up tech companies in Silicon Valley. Being in on the ground floor of something new and exciting was enough to engage many employees. But then, as the company grew and became more of an institution, things changed. The culture and demands of a start-up company clashed with the needs of employees wanting a work/life balance, less stress, a sense of belonging and worth, and fair treatment in a huge corporation with thousands of employees.

Amazon started receiving criticism for the way it treated its employees, especially in its warehouse fulfillment centers, where many positions were lower-wage, minimally skilled jobs. Although Amazon paid well and offered good benefits, its business model focused on using technology to increase productivity, bottom-line results, and delivering flawlessly on customer demand. The goal was to be able to deliver goods anywhere in record time. The employees working at the warehouses were viewed as a part of this production process. High productivity quotas were set, and employees were constantly monitored to make sure these quotas were met. A point-demerit system was used to weed out underperformers who were, for example, late too many times.

Former employees reported leaving their jobs at Amazon because the environment was so high-stress that they had little time even for bathroom breaks. They felt extreme mental and physical pressure that didn't let up. On-the-job injuries were frequent. They said that Amazon put vending machines in its facilities with ibuprofen and other over-the-counter pain medications to decrease the number of people waiting in line to see the company's nurse.

In its defense, Amazon argued that these complaints came from a small minority of disgruntled workers out of the 300,000 people employed in these areas. They pointed out that the company paid higher salaries, offered more full-time jobs, and paid benefits that their competitors didn't as proof that their employees were being treated well.

In their November 2021 report *Reveal,* The Center for Investigative Reporting said that they looked at 23 out of Amazon's 110 fulfillment centers nationwide. They found that Amazon's rate of serious injuries was 9.6 serious injuries per 100 full-time workers in 2018, more than double the national average of four in the warehousing industry. Amazon's response was that their numbers were higher because Amazon was more diligent about reporting injuries than other companies.

At the same time, Amazon's turnover rates suggested that perhaps employees weren't as satisfied as Amazon was claiming. In mid-2021, the *New York Times* reported that, even before the pandemic, Amazon's turnover rate for hourly employees was 150% or about a 3% turnover a week, nearly double the rate of similar businesses. This meant that Amazon essentially replaced its entire hourly warehouse workforce every eight months.

New York Times reporter Jodi Kantor explained that part of the reason for this turnover was that Jeff Bezos, founder of Amazon and then CEO, had designed turnover on purpose into their business model. "He envisioned Amazon as like the Marine Corps: You would come for two years, it would be really hard, and then you would move on. So, turnover is almost built into the system. If you look at the way they pay, they just don't expect to keep people for very long. And also, promotion is very limited. Hourly workers get really excited to join Amazon because they feel like they're going to be a part of something very successful. However, it is very hard to fully participate in the success of the company, beyond the good wages and good benefits, because it's very hard to move up."

One of the things that allowed Amazon to ramp up so quickly during the pandemic and to continue to grow rapidly was its approach to its workforce. Instead of using people to do many human-resource functions, Amazon uses technology. For example, they have a fully automated "lights-out hiring" process. A candidate isn't interviewed by a person; they take an online assessment, and besides filling out some basic forms and taking a drug test, are hired based solely on that. They are not interviewed by a person. Once on the job, employees' performance and productivity are measured and monitored primarily through technology, not by managers physically observing them. This means that, for about every 100 employees, there is only one manager. You can see why promotion opportunities are limited. And this automated approach is true for most of the human-resource processes at Amazon, including performance reviews and firing.

It's no wonder that Amazon employees have complained about feeling disposable; some even suggested that the bots at Amazon were treated better than they were. Consistently, employees said they didn't like the constant monitoring or not being able to talk to someone about HR issues. Just think about how frustrating automated phone systems are. Then imagine *that* being your experience every day at work.

While other companies across the globe are trying to move to a more empathetic paradigm of doing business, Amazon seems to be moving in the other direction—by removing as much human contact as possible.

During the pandemic, with many people looking for work, Amazon was able to hire without having to worry too much about its high turnover and injury rates. But in 2021, employees became much more vocal. Some Amazon warehouses attempted to bring unions in. These are not the actions of happily engaged workers. In addition, the labor market tightened, and Amazon had to raise wages and institute only limited screening for marijuana to entice more applicants. Given these trends, some people question whether Amazon can sustain its current business model—turning over its entire workforce every eight months—and still grow. In 2020, the company spent $44 billion in capital investments in anticipation of future growth, some of which will be new warehouses that will need to be staffed. The question remains: Can Amazon sustain a business model which gives little heed to engaging its workforce, and still compete in the labor market of the future?

The leadership of the company has acknowledged it should humanize its human resources. In mid-2021, just before stepping down as CEO, Jeff Bezos pledged that he wanted Amazon to become Earth's best employer. But more than a year later, there is little evidence that much has significantly improved. In October 2022, confidential documents were leaked showing employee turnover still at 150%, which costs the company and its shareholders $8 billion a year. Although Amazon has cast doubt on the leaked documents' accuracy, given its history and lack of evidence of real change, the numbers aren't hard to believe.

This business model affects not only the distribution workers but has repercussions also for higher-level jobs. A few Target executives I knew left to go to Amazon and then came back to Target. Amazon had dangled huge signing bonuses in front of them to lure them away. They'd returned because Amazon's approach had been intensity on steroids, everything focused on nonstop productivity and results, with little else taken into consideration. My colleagues quickly decided it wasn't the kind of work environment they wanted.

In 2011, about five months before I retired from the Army and started working for Target, I was recruited by Amazon. They've always had a pretty aggressive program to hire former military. I went to visit one of their fulfillment centers in Columbia, South Carolina. It was a fairly new facility, and I visited with its leader about two days before Christmas. I was told that, if I were hired, the plan was that I'd run a facility for a while and then move on to bigger and better things.

The leader of the facility looked like the walking dead—dark circles under his eyes, a weary appearance, completely run-down. They had just finished their holiday seasonal rush, and he was wiped out, having worked 18-hour days for about two months. He talked frankly to me about how grueling it was.

Later, I thought about that haggard facility leader, after I'd gone through holiday peak periods with Target. My team had also worked longer hours than normal, but we hadn't come out of it as exhausted as that man looked. I couldn't help thinking the difference had something to do with engagement and how devalued Amazon's employees felt. It couldn't have just been the monitoring technology. All companies have systems to monitor employee productivity, including Target, but how those systems are used and what is done with employees who aren't hitting their numbers definitely make a difference. I thought, of course, it would have been exhausting for that director! Managing a staff from a distance without much human interaction doesn't offer managers much of the "good stuff," either.

What it comes down to, in my opinion, is that, even though Amazon is offering good pay and benefits, and the prestige of working for an innovator, they are woefully lacking in providing employees what really matters to them: opportunities for advancement, respect, acknowledgment of their contributions, being cared about, and being told the reasons why. In other words, the all-important human connection.

Amazon's business model suggests that this human connection needs to be sacrificed to maximize productivity and results. But it doesn't have to be that way. Getting results and connecting to subordinates are not mutually exclusive. In fact, I would argue they are the yin and the yang.

Good organizations hold leaders accountable for *both* bottom-line results and employee engagement. Target did this with its annual Best Team Survey, which was a voluntary survey all team members were asked to take. If a leader's participation rate was below 90% for their facility, they had to answer for it, because non-participation is often a sign of disengagement. Having high participation rates, however, didn't mean leaders didn't have to get results and meet productivity goals.

Instead of being at odds, the two go hand-in-hand. I saw this in the Army as well. Good senior leaders in the Army spent time with soldiers at levels below them, were in tune with the tone of their unit, devoted time to mentoring subordinates, and cared. And they more than met their objectives. Their units always stood above the rest. Abusive and toxic leaders did the opposite, and invariably their units were mediocre at best. Engagement drives results, not the other way around.

I think one of the reasons some leaders think engagement and bottom-line results are mutually exclusive is because they believe engagement happens when subordinates like their bosses, and a leader who is a pal with subordinates lets "the inmates run the show." But being liked and having engaged subordinates are not the same thing. Engagement isn't a popularity contest. Leaders who want to be liked at the expense of holding subordinates accountable will not have any better luck at creating an engaged workforce than superiors who are not liked at all.

When I commanded a brigade combat team, I was a stickler for vehicle-load plans for all combat vehicles, such as tanks. A load plan was a specific, detailed plan of where everything should go—spare ammunition, first-aid kit, spare machine-gun barrels, repair parts, ancillary equipment, and fire extinguishers. The reason these plans were so important was to make sure that any tank crewman in the brigade could jump on a tank and know exactly where everything was located. In the middle of a combat situation, nobody wants to be searching around for a first-aid kit if a wounded soldier is bleeding out.

During my second year of command, a new battalion commander, Gene, took command of a tank battalion in my brigade. One day, I conducted an inspection of his tank battalion, specifically to check load plans. I noticed discrepancies. Given all my harping on the subject, I was surprised.

"Gene, did you notice these discrepancies?" I asked.

"Well, sir, you've been clear about your intent to have all load plans the same," he said. "But my company commanders had some ideas, and I thought it was important to let them use their own initiative, roll on their own a bit."

I looked at him. He was a new battalion commander, and he wanted to make a good impression on his subordinates. He wanted them to like him. He was giving them the freedom to do it their way.

I frowned. "Have them fix it. I'll be back to check that it's done, and then we need to have a talk."

Later that day, I called him into my office. I reiterated my rationale for insisting on consistent load plans. I told him I understood that he wanted his team to like him. Every new commander does.

"But part of your job as a leader is to enforce these standards, Gene," I said. "Your soldiers will respect you more if you hold them to high standards, tell them why you're doing so, and train the hell out of them. Keep raising the bar. If you let things slide because you think they won't like you if your bar is too high, you'll be doing everyone a disservice. It's all in how you communicate the standard and why it's important."

We went on to discuss that leaders need to understand which things are flexible and which are not. For the things that can't be changed, they need to be able to articulate why. I told him it was kind of like building a house. Some things must be built to code. That's not a place where deviation should be encouraged. Creativity comes with what you build around those specifications. Giving subordinates specifications and having them understand why they exist makes their job less stressful. It allows them to focus creative energy on the things that can be changed.

He nodded. We didn't have to have that discussion again.

The point is every organization has its "codes." These can be productivity goals, safety standards, or compliance policies— whatever is non-negotiable. Just because a leader needs to enforce them doesn't mean leaders can't also have a personal relationship with subordinates and be empathetic. Simply being "liked" shows only that you are congenial. Employee engagement means just that—*engaging* employees in the conversation, whatever it may be.

The other myth that leaders tell themselves is that working on employee engagement takes up too much time. It's one more thing on the to-do list. And I get it. The tasks of any leader in any organization may seem innumerable and endless. There are always more things that need to get done than there is time to do them.

But too often, leaders hunker down in their offices and busy themselves with paperwork, reports, and analyzing data, and spend only a minority of their time with their subordinates. In reality, it should be the opposite. Remember, the main job of a leader is to *get things done through others*. Investing time in employees helps ensure that happens. Think again about building a house. What would happen if you gathered a team together and said, "Here are some architectural drawings and specs. I'd like you to build me a house in a month, and I'll check with you when you're done." You send them off without establishing a relationship with them other than knowing whatever skill they bring to the project. You don't interact with them while they build the house except to question why they have worked so many overtime hours or gone over budget. What is the likelihood that you will be happy with that house? What is the likelihood that the team would want to work under those conditions?

What makes work undertaken by a group successful is the interaction between the members of the group—again, *the human connection*. As the leader, while you are also a team member, your main responsibility is to make these connections happen. It starts with you. And one of the best ways to make a connection with another human being is to allow yourself to be vulnerable.

Here is what leaders must do to have engaged employees:

1. Get to know your employees.

2. Make sure they understand what they're doing and have the tools to do it.

3. Make sure they understand why they're doing things and how they fit into the big picture.

4. Give them opportunities to grow professionally and personally; let them show they can lead.

5. Back them up when you give them authority.

6. Listen to them, and act on their feedback.

7. Encourage teamwork and camaraderie.

8. Recognize contributions and hard work.

9. Create an open, inclusive environment, free of fear.

10. Be a coach and a cheerleader; motivate and inspire.

But these are just words unless leaders are willing to do the most important thing that underlies all 10 directives: be vulnerable. None of these things can be successfully accomplished without leaders being willing to take a hard look at themselves and be honest about what they see—to admit that they don't have all the answers and that they need help, to understand their own limitations, to be willing to give up control, to put themselves in someone else's shoes—all the things we've talked about in the preceding chapters. Engaged workforces don't happen any other way.

I took the job at Target before going any further in the process with Amazon. And I'm glad I did. Knowing what I do now, I can tell Amazon wouldn't have been a good fit for me. Most people, including me, want a job that feels like a second home, a place where we're appreciated. We crave human connection.

As a leader, you can provide that for your employees. You simply have to do one thing.

Be vulnerable.

‹ ◄ ◆ ► ›

CONCLUSION

Vulnerability has always been part of the human condition. What's new is the idea that it doesn't have to be hidden or relegated to the realm of victimhood. Exhibiting it in an intentional way can improve all aspects of our lives and deepen the human connections we make. Having gone on the journey from a scripted and enforced view of what leadership looks like in the Army to an understanding of the value of vulnerability for all leaders, I have grown as a human being and leader.

I see signs that I am not the only one, that our society as a whole is becoming more open to the idea that leaders who are "large and in charge" are not the ideal leadership role models anymore.

In September 2020, Air Force General John Hyten, Vice Chairman of the Joint Chiefs of Staff, went public about his mental health issues to encourage all service members to seek help if they were struggling with thoughts of suicide or other psychological conditions. He said when he was the commander of US Strategic Command, he'd gone to a therapist for help. "I got an appointment with a psychiatrist; I was kindly offered anonymous, backdoor entry, and I rejected it. If I'd had the flu, I'd walk through the front door to see the doctor. This was no different. Our mental and physical health are equal in importance . . . I got the help I needed, and I'm stronger for it."

This kind of admission by a senior military leader would have been unheard of a decade ago, but suicide rates are climbing in the military. In 2019, the Veterans Administration reported that about 20 veterans and active-duty service members die from suicide *each day*. General Hyten was willing to show personal vulnerability in an attempt to diminish the stigma of mental health challenges and help others.

I am certain that General Hyten didn't plan on letting the world know he'd sought professional mental health treatment. But the situation arose where, by doing so, he could contribute to a wider population who needed to hear his message. Part of being a vulnerable leader is recognizing opportunities that will make a difference and then allowing oneself to be vulnerable despite fear, possible repercussions, or backlash. The end goal is to help or empower *someone else.*

When leaders show this type of vulnerability, people respond because it establishes common ground and acknowledges our similarities as humans. It allows others to peek under the tent flap of who we are. It gives them a glimpse, just enough to create a bond—there's no need to invite them to move into the tent. These bonds are the basis for all relationships, for creating work that is meaningful.

We've talked a lot throughout this book about different aspects of vulnerability, how it helps leaders develop, promote, and create engaged employees, and how it ultimately makes everyone more successful. But, if I had to boil it down to the two most important things leaders must show in order to be vulnerable leaders, it would be self-awareness and empathy.

Leaders can't simply wake up one day and claim to be vulnerable; they can't decide whether they've been vulnerable in this interaction or that. It doesn't work that way. Like anything that requires authenticity, only *others* can *attribute* vulnerability *to* us. We have to be honest with ourselves and listen to what others say. We must understand what it's like for the other people we impact.

I retired from Target in 2019, not because I didn't love my job, but to help my wife realize her dream of getting her PhD and working at a college or university in her field of nutrition. She'd sacrificed so much for me, and it was my turn to support her. Her plan was to defend her doctoral dissertation no later than October 2019, graduate in December, and begin looking for an academic position. We would move wherever she found work, and I would find flexible part-time work.

All went according to plan, except she hadn't bargained that the search for a professorship would be such a challenge. She knew her age might count against her, but the Covid pandemic hit in the middle of her search, upending everything. While she continued to search, we decided that, instead of waiting to see where she might find a job, we'd sell our home in Illinois and buy a home in Denver, where both of our sons lived and where we planned to eventually retire.

While getting our house ready to sell, however, my wife received fabulous news. She'd been offered a position at North Central College in Naperville, Illinois, to be the program director in nutrition science, a new major for the college. She'd be developing the program from the ground up, as well as teaching classes—more than she'd hoped for.

But this meant we were committed to spending at least half of the year in Illinois. We decided to go ahead and buy a house in Denver and rent a house in Naperville. We would split our time between the two places.

Immediately, this brought up some issues for me. There is one corner of my life where I am a control freak, and that has to do with maintaining a house. I like everything taken care of and in working order. With traveling back and forth from Illinois to Denver, I wouldn't be full-time at our new home, and that made me uncomfortable. I'm a worrier. What if things break down, water pipes burst, furnaces or air conditioning go on the fritz, and I'm not there? I worried about these things out loud.

Whenever I brought up my concerns about the house with Kim, while she understood—as she always does—I also sensed my apprehensions caused her stress. She was committed to what she was doing, excited about the program she was developing, and she didn't need or want to deal with my "house anxiety."

It made me stop and think. Because maintaining a house was important to me, admittedly overly so, I was assuming they were as important to her. I realized that it was *my* issue, not *hers*. Why was I burdening her with it? Trying to make her feel guilty? I admitted to her that I was being selfish in wanting her to focus on my concerns. I stopped bringing it up. Figuring out how to manage the house long distance or make the best of the situation was my problem to solve. I got comfortable with being uncomfortable about the house.

But this interaction made me realize that all my work on becoming a more vulnerable leader had changed me as a person. It made me so much more self-aware and empathetic. And it had spilled over into the rest of my life. Instead of blindly pushing forward my agenda on our house, I had stopped and listened to my wife's nonverbal cues. In examining myself, I'd acknowledged that the problem was mine, not my wife's. I had put myself into her shoes and realized how unfair it was of me to expect her to do anything about my anxiety.

This, then, is the gift of striving to become a more vulnerable leader. It makes you more in tune with yourself and others. And the world could use a lot more of that.

‹ ‹ ◆ › ›

ABOUT THE AUTHORS

Major General (Retired) Mike Milano is a leadership trainer and consultant with 44 years of experience leading at all organizational levels, both in the United States Army and in corporate America. After a brilliant 33-year career in the Army leading troops in several operational and combat deployments and commanding two premier installations, he spent seven years with Target Corporation in field leadership positions.

Holly Richmond is a writer with an MFA in creative writing from the University of Nebraska. For almost 20 years, she worked as a marketing executive in the banking and insurance industry, much of that time spent with a Fortune 500 company.

APPENDIX I

Milano's 15 Principles of Vulnerable Leadership

1. Vulnerability is the building block of good leadership.

2. A vulnerable leader doesn't have to know everything.

3. Vulnerability doesn't live in your comfort zone.

4. Vulnerability can close the cultural divide.

5. Fear makes us vulnerable; embracing it makes us powerful.

6. Vulnerability requires a will to learn.

7. Vulnerability is opportunity's wingman.

8. Vulnerability is the link between trust and loyalty.

9. Vulnerability means harnessing emotion.

10. Good feedback is an act of vulnerability on both sides.

11. Vulnerable leaders enable others and leave a human legacy.

12. Vulnerability enables empathy, the basis for caring.

13. The art of vulnerability is the language of communication.

14. There's no faking vulnerability.

15. Vulnerability makes human connection blossom.

APPENDIX II

Do You Know Your Limitations?

1. **When I ask a question, are people reluctant to answer?** When people think you want to hear only one thing, they will resist answering until they have a sense of what you're looking for.

2. **How many times do I ask for input from others in meetings?** If you are not looking for others' ideas or opinions, you might as well not have a meeting. You already know the answer.

3. **What is the motivation for my behavior?** Am I doing this to further something, or am I doing it to be right or prove my brilliance?

4. **Have I sought honest feedback from subordinates and peers about ways that I can improve my effectiveness?** If yes, then what have I done with that feedback? If no, then why not?

APPENDIX III

Do's & Don'ts of Feedback

Do's

1. Describe the specific behavior that needs to change, and do so without using judgment—just the facts. Using verbs rather than adjectives helps. *She didn't listen to the client's request* instead of *She was impatient.*

2. Focus on what *you noticed* about the behavior, not on what others might have said about it.

3. Be clear about the message you are delivering without vacillating, rambling, being vague, talking in circles, speaking on behalf of others, or muddying up the message with other tactics.

Don'ts

1. Don't judge the person. Focus on their behaviors—on what they *did.*

2. Don't use clichés or vague phrases that leave the person wondering what the feedback refers to, such as *You're an ace.*

3. Don't sandwich negative feedback between positive statements.

4. Don't generalize with words like "always" or "never." It creates defensiveness.

5. Don't go on and on. People stop listening, and it devalues the feedback.

6. Don't make yourself a psychologist and attempt to explain someone's behavior.

7. Don't ever use feedback as a subtle threat. *If you don't get with the program . . .*

8. Don't pose feedback as a rhetorical question that suggests behavioral change is optional. *Do you think you might . . . ?*

9. Don't inject humor or use sarcasm.

10. Don't bring your own emotional baggage into the conversation.

APPENDIX IV

Assessing Your Vulnerability Authenticity

Context:

1. Consider the purpose of the interaction/event/meeting, the people attending, and your role and responsibilities before you share.

2. Consider whether what you have to share belongs in the public or private sphere.

3. If you have been talking more than listening, consider stepping back and listening until you fully grasp the situation or context.

4. Given the occasion, have you set clear boundaries?

5. Is what you're sharing something that will produce a result or move the conversation forward?

Trust

1. Has sufficient trust been established with the person or group?

2. Are you aware of the hierarchy of power dynamics that is present? Trust on a peer level is not the same as trust between leader and subordinate.

3. Are you prepared for negative feedback? Rarely with large groups will you have established 100% trust, so you will need to accept that not everyone may believe in your sincerity.

Motivation

1. Consider whether you have an agenda—what do you hope to gain from sharing?

2. Are you looking for a way to excuse your bad behavior or set up a defense?

3. Are you one-upping someone else's sharing? "If you think *that's* bad . . ." Are you being empathic and really listening or eager to share only your own experiences?

4. Has your sharing resulted in a real connection? If not, look deeper for your underlying motivation.